If you want to:

- Learn how to use energetic self healing to clear pain and trauma

- Increase your own sense of unconditional self-love

- Develop inner confidence and inner strength

- Use mindfulness wisely in all of your activities

- Create a beneficial energetic alignment in your own being that will increase your ability to help the planet

Then this is the book for you!

Walking the Soul Path

An Energetic Guide to Being Human

Using Energetic Self Healing to Go Beyond the Mind to Transform Ourselves and the World

Includes 18 Energetic Self Healing Techniques

Ruth Lera

Self Healing Community Press

www.ruthlera.com

Copyright (c)2017 by Ruth Lera

First edition – 2017

Photo Credits:

Cover: Pexels.com (CCO license)

Author Photo: Cathie Archbould Photography

ISBN: 978-1-7751113-0-6

In the course of this great spiral, we return to where we started again and again but each time with a fuller, more open heart.

-Jack Kornfield-

Table of Contents

Alphabetical List of Energetic Self Healing Techniques

Introduction

Human existence is intrinsically difficult.

This piece of information shouldn't come as a shock to anyone presently living in human form.

We all know that life is challenging. We know this because we all encounter discomfort in some form each and every day.

This suffering is not something to be taken lightly. It is painful and hard to handle, but it's also our greatest opportunity.

This paradox of *hating* our suffering while simultaneously *needing* our suffering is the most meaningful challenge each of us is facing right now. How to best manoeuvre through this paradox is guidance we can all use.

Our soul's path is made up of basic daily choices in which we simultaneously try to reduce our suffering while striving to be of benefit to ourselves and the greater community we are a part of.

When we understand that we can open wider to all the goodness of our soul's path by allowing our challenges to be opportunities, we find ourselves able to float on the current of life, weathering the ups and downs with a full heart. This seems like a better choice

than always feeling like a victim to life, constantly swimming upstream against every frustration.

How to do this isn't always obvious, though. At least, it hasn't been for me.

Most people who know me see me as a confident person, but the truth is confusion has been my constant companion. Fortunately, my naïve attempt to try to 'fix' the uncomfortable feelings that accompany my constant sense of uncertainty has led me to explore my own relationship with my mind, heart, soul path, and energy.

This all started for me at age 18. I was living in a small, rural village in northeastern Thailand, on a Canada World Youth exchange, when I realized that even though I was halfway around the world, I didn't really feel any different than I had when I was living at my parents' house in Toronto.

Wasn't going to a new place supposed to make me feel better? This had been my expectation when I left for Thailand. However, early on in the trip I saw that changing physical locations wasn't curing my suffering as I had hoped it would.

It turned out that leaving Toronto was not the same thing as leaving myself.

I was living in another country but I was still living with myself, which meant I still had to deal with all the neurosis, loneliness and

confusion inside of me. This part of my being that suffered had followed me halfway around the world.

It was then that I was forced to acknowledge that I wasn't ever going to be able to travel far enough that I would successfully run away from myself.

The only choice I had was to stop running, sit down and face myself.

The realization that my suffering was an inside job led me to start exploring the teachings of the Buddha, and this was exactly what his teachings were pointing to. The fact that life is suffering, but also that we can alleviate this suffering when we learn how to work effectively with it. And that the most effective way to do this is through meditation.

When I returned to Toronto I started a meditation practice and immediately felt the profound results of sitting in silence undisturbed with my own breath.

I started to feel calmer and connected to a Universal consciousness I previously hadn't believed even existed. But instead of continuing this practice, I did what most of us do when we know something is good for us—I avoided it for the better part of a decade.

During that time, I was completely caught up in the stress of being in a monogamous relationship with another human, and eventually

a parent to two young children. The pressures of trying to pay my bills and figure out my life purpose took the place of my meditation practice.

I started meditating seriously again in my early thirties, after I attended a silent meditation retreat. I chose to attend the retreat in an attempt to overcome my challenges at the time, which were basically that my life was totally out of control.

By out of control I mean that I felt like I couldn't cope. I often found myself mid-day clutching the kitchen sink and wondering, "How the heck am I going to get through this day?" I knew I needed to start doing something differently.

The teachings I received at the meditation retreat watered the seeds of awareness inside of me. I began to understand how we can work with our suffering to bring greater benefit to ourselves and everyone around us. It never occurred to me that one day I would be instructing others in the practice of meditation. But that is eventually what happened.

As meditation became an integral part of my own life, I realized that sharing meditation with others would be the best way I could make my own life meaningful. I trained in meditation and mindfulness instruction and began teaching people in my local community how to meditate through courses I designed. I also

began studying different modalities of energy healing, such as Healing Touch and Quantum Touch.

The combination of studying energy healing modalities and meditating regularly transformed me. I learned that by limiting the attention I gave to my thoughts, I could then give my attention to other aspects of my conscious experience, such as sensing energy for the purpose of creating a healing response for myself and others.

In 2013, I began conducting private energy healing sessions in person and eventually by distance with people worldwide. I love these private energy healing sessions for the pure joy of connection they provide in my life.

But even after conducting nearly a thousand energy healing sessions, and observing clients experience profound improvements in every area of their lives, I felt like I wanted to offer more. I wanted to teach people how to practice energetic healing on themselves.

The foundation of energetic self healing is the knowledge that everything that happens in our lives affects our energy, and everything in our energy affects our lives. Therefore, by having the skills to heal our energy, we can engage in daily self healing choices as a direct means of maintaining our holistic health.

When we are energetically aligned, the rest of our life flows more freely.

This is why I created *The Self Healing Community*: an online portal for people to learn energetic self healing techniques. We all need help learning how to work with our minds and our suffering. We all need guidance to learn how to move our attention to our energy so we can shift it into a the most fulfilling position possible.

The techniques for energetic self healing are simple, but we don't always know how to start. This is why I have put all the resources and support you need in order to practice energetic self healing in one location - *The Self Healing Community*.

The most empowering choice we can make on our soul path is choosing what information is being stored within our own energy.

When we have the skills to clear energetic information that is no longer needed out of our systems, and let new life force energy flow in naturally, we will find ourselves feeling more grounded and more accepting. We will find that our life experience is filled with increased compassion, ease, and joy.

I wrote this book because I want to share my view on why we experience suffering, and how we can work with it skillfully through self-awareness, meditation, and energetic self healing for the purpose of transforming our challenges into soul path opportunity.

Maybe this seems impossible? Maybe it seems like your suffering will always be with you, because it *has* always been with you. But we don't want to let the past dictate the future! The belief that you can't heal yourself is just another piece of energetic misinformation stored in your energy causing you unnecessary suffering.

The good news is you don't need to become a monk, yogi, or spiritually obsessed person to start healing yourself from the inside out. The point of these teachings and techniques is that they are actually meant to be used on a very mundane level. You can use them from the comfort of your home, while washing the dishes, walking the dog, or just lying in bed.

You don't even need to devote much time to these techniques; the point is to just practice energetic self healing to the best of your ability on a regular basis. These techniques will be most beneficial for you when you commit to making them part of your regular self-care practice.

If you spend even a few minutes a day using these techniques, you will be grateful that you did. They will bring you an increased clarity about what you need to do in order to manage life's challenges.

What I'm about to share with you is not new information. It's ancient knowledge in much need of resurrection. You, and every other human on this planet, have the precious opportunity to embody a human form. Just this basic reality of being human

allows you to courageously develop your capacity to love while simultaneously thriving on a personal level and contributing to the healing of the planet, but only if you choose to.

I hope this reality is as exciting to you as it is to me.

Let's get started!

Chapter One

Life is Suffering

Saying that life is suffering may not seem very helpful. At first glance, it may seem overly pessimistic. I mean, really, who wants to think about suffering? The truth is mostly people don't.

suf·fer·ing: the state of undergoing pain, distress, or hardship

We don't want to think about suffering, our own or others, because we equate suffering with a sense of depression and hopelessness. We have a habit of trying to avoid anything to do with suffering.

But I would like to propose that it's possible to take a more optimistic stance on suffering. What if our capacity to accept suffering as a natural part of life is what actually allows us the ability to open to a greater sense of ease and joy in our lives? What if the simple act of choosing to look at suffering from a new perspective could in itself ease the suffering?

When we don't acknowledge that the innate reality of human life is suffering, and we then find ourselves in a continual state of emotional, mental, physical, and spiritual pain, we end up blaming

1

ourselves (and others) for our discomfort. We enter into this cycle of blame because we think we aren't supposed to suffer. We think we are messing up in some way when suffering is present. This idea that our suffering is a sign that we are messing up is in fact one of the main ways we suffer.

Confused yet? Let me explain further.

When we believe we aren't meant to suffer, but then do, we become convinced that our suffering is our own fault. We end up hurting ourselves even more through the way we talk to ourselves about the frustrations and disappointments we are experiencing.

Blaming ourselves for our pain is a special type of cruelty that most of us know all too well. In some form all of us are engaging in this type of self-blame for the suffering we experience, though most of us don't even realize we're doing this.

Suffering is not a sign that we are doing anything wrong or are being bad in any way. It is simply a normal part of being human.

The acknowledgement that being human means we will undoubtedly experience suffering is a beneficial awareness we can embrace for the simple reason that it will help us suffer less. If we are truly committed to benefiting ourselves and others, it is essential that we understand that suffering is the norm.

We are all born, we all have challenges along the way and we all die. We all experience this truth. In this way, we are all the same.

Look at your life. There is no denying there have been moments that have been really hard for you. You have experienced disappointments, confusions, big losses, little losses, grief, and pain. You have been hurt by others, and have been the perpetrator of pain, probably even to people you love. Even right now you may be experiencing an ongoing sense of anxiety or doubt about how to create a life that feels safe, secure, and happy.

How do I know this? Because we are all human and we all feel this way. In the realm of experiencing pain and challenge, we are all the same. We all experience pain, and we all wish it would end when it's occurring.

Many people would disagree with what I've just stated. Many people would believe it's possible to live a painless life that completely prevents suffering if the correct choices were made.

Also, to many people it probably seems like some of us experience much worse suffering than others. If you look around the globe and observe people's qualities of life, the discrepancies are blatantly obvious. It is impossible to ignore the fact that some people are experiencing terrible suffering, and others are living a life of comfort. But perhaps this isn't the entire picture?

If we start to look past the outside appearance of people's situations we see that it doesn't matter how fortunate someone's life is, everyone is experiencing challenge, pain, and difficulty in one form or another on their human journey.

Now, of course, some people do live in war zones and some people do live in mansions and it would seem like the life of someone living in a war zone is much worse than the life of someone living in a mansion, and this is true.

Some pain is much worse than others. There is unbelievable brutality in the world, and the pain experienced in these situations is unjust. No one deserves to live or die in atrocious situations such as war or famine.

It is also true that every human, no matter how seemingly fortunate their physical life circumstance is, experiences feelings of loneliness, abandonment, and inadequacy.

The realization that everyone is hurting in some way can be incredibly disheartening, but only if we choose to believe that we have no power to use our pain for good.

One thing that prevents us from transforming our pain is the feeling of powerlessness that arises when we are faced with global suffering. We might find ourselves wondering: Is there any way to put an end to the global pain and suffering that is occurring?

Well, of course, the answer is no. We aren't going to end all child poverty, stop every war, or alleviate all global suffering in this lifetime.

But that doesn't mean we aren't going to alleviate *any* suffering.

When we skillfully work with our suffering, we find out that we *can* heal much of the personal pain we are experiencing—and this has a global impact.

When we don't push our suffering away but instead let it be part of our lives, we become softened by the experience of our suffering. When we regularly practice being compassionate towards the suffering we experience, the loving energy we develop touches every person we meet.

Sakyong Mipham, head of the Shambhala Buddhist lineage explains it like this:

> "Self-reflection is how we can transform society. Transforming society happens one person at a time, by our willingness to be kind to ourselves, and our willingness to be kind to one another."

It takes commitment and a strong level of self-awareness to turn our suffering into healing, but millions of people around the world are doing it as we speak. Realising that we are a part of a collective

community working towards healing can be a great source of support.

If this is a commitment you are ready to make, then the most important thing you need to realize about working skillfully with your suffering is that it isn't a conceptual experience. It's not something you're going to fully understand intellectually or be able to accomplish through thinking about it.

It is something you have to *do*.

Getting too intellectual about our experience of healing pain and working with suffering is the perfect way to avoid getting down to the actual work of transforming pain and suffering into a powerful growth opportunity.

That is why, as you go through this book, I encourage you not to ask too many existential questions about why your suffering exists and instead focus on getting intimate with what you're actually experiencing in your mind, heart, body, and energy.

As you explore what it means to be on a soul path, and as you learn how to energetically heal your pain and trauma, you will need to draw on your courage, willingness, and ability to connect with your present experience with all of your senses.

The healing techniques offered in this book are simple to use but the process of accepting suffering and intentionally changing our

energetic patterns is not necessarily an easy task. You will likely notice some real resistance through this process, and if you don't bring a friendly attitude of love and kindness with you on your healing journey, you might find yourself feeling increasingly weaker instead of more empowered.

However, before we get into specific energetic self healing techniques, we are going to discuss the foundational principles of what it means to be a soul walking a long path, and how we all have the capacity to heal ourselves every step of the way.

Chapter Two

What Does It Mean to Walk the Soul Path?

When I say that we are walking the soul path, what I am referring to is the concept that we are long-living souls only temporarily inhabiting this human body we call the self.

soul: the spiritual or immaterial part of a human being or animal, regarded as immortal

Some of us wish we didn't have to be who we are, but wishing we weren't living the life we presently have is the epitome of human suffering. No matter how much we may want to, we can't go back and choose to not be born as the person we are.

When we spend our energy wishing that we weren't experiencing suffering as the person we presently are, we disregard the great potential that is available to us as souls inhabiting this particular human experience.

Regarding ourselves as souls having a human experience, rather than just being a random, purposeless body, helps us gain a greater understanding of our present situation, while also providing us with a feeling of being a part of an interconnected Universe beyond what we know.

I'd like to propose that, with the intention of healing ourselves, you try to think of your soul as something that chose to incarnate into your present human body because it had things it wanted to learn and experience.

The person you are now is a representation of many lessons, experiences, and energetic alignments that your soul has accumulated through many incarnations.

Generally, these aren't lessons or experiences we have a conscious recollection of, but for whatever reason, we have chosen to once again have a human experience to continue with the soul lessons we began in previous lives.

The main challenge is that now that you're here as a human, what you've probably found out is that the experience of being human can be hard, confusing, full of suffering, and very difficult to understand.

It can also be blissful, full of joy, and incredibly fulfilling!

This opportunity to be human is an incredibly substantial and illuminating experience for your soul's development. When you become aware that your soul purposely chose to be in this human form, you start to see that being the person you are is not something to be taken for granted.

> Acknowledging that we are a soul having a human experience increases our healing potential.

If we assume that being our present human self is pointless, we discount our greatness and minimize the sense of meaning this life can offer.

The challenge we all have is that there is no way to find out exactly what our present soul purpose is; and this lack of obvious answers to why we are here can be the hardest part of whole process.

If there was a pill we could take or a button we could push to help us learn our soul's lessons instantly and end our suffering, and the suffering of others, I would be the first one doing the swallowing and pushing…but there isn't.

And it's a good thing that there aren't any magical solutions to ending our human pain, because our soul needs challenges to develop. This is what we come to understand when we embrace walking the soul path; that we've incarnated as a human for the purpose of experiencing challenges which will help heal soul pain created in the past. The soul lessons we cultivate in this present life are what we will take with us through future soul incarnations.

But what does this all really mean? Does it even matter that we are souls in the end? Well, yes it does matter because when we embrace our soul nature it makes it easier for us to accept that our suffering isn't pointless. In fact all of our experiences are incredibly

11

meaningful, as they are the opportunities provided to us for the purpose of developing our soul's capacity to learn and love.

Each challenge we face is an opportunity to choose how we react to life. For instance, if we feel like we have no confidence, then we are being given an opportunity to learn how to have confidence. If we are feeling alone, we are being given the opportunity to learn how not to feel alone.

All situations that make us feel negative about ourselves are opportunities to learn how to believe in ourselves. Put very simply, walking the soul path allows us to transform our limitations into opportunities for growth.

However, consistently putting into action this understanding that our challenges are soul opportunities can feel very difficult. Still the concept is quite simple— you are a human in the here and now because your soul has things it wants to learn and develop.

Dr. Brian L. Weiss in his book *Many Lives, Many Masters* explains it this way:

> "Our body is just a vehicle for us while we're here.
> It is our soul and our spirit that last forever."

Being open to the concept of being an eternal soul offers us access to greater healing for the simple reason that much of what we experience in our lives is a mystery.

It is extremely hard to understand why we are the way we are, and this can be a source of frustration for many. When we are willing to look at our soul as an eternal entity that holds information from past lives, we find a new perspective on life and new answers to our challenges often emerge in unexpected ways.

Walking the soul path is the way in which we stop feeling like a victim every time life doesn't go our way. When we get fired from a job, get our hearts broken, or are diagnosed with an illness that changes the quality of our life, we often feel like we're being punished. But perhaps we are being given specific circumstances to develop something our soul needs.

We will never know for sure what we are meant to learn as a soul in this particular, unique body, but walking the soul path means making an effort to try to find out.

Becoming aware and open to the reality of being a soul in a human body provides the opportunity to be increasingly aware of the soul impact each has on our greater journey.

We will never walk our soul path in one, big step, though. Instead the soul path consists of every single, little step we take. Every single one!

Chapter Three

Do We Need to Believe in Past Lives to Walk the Soul Path?

Perhaps you find the notion of reincarnation or some sort of afterlife reassuring, believing that you and your loved ones will meet again after death. Or perhaps you find the concept of reincarnation ridiculous, and are unable to accept that any part of us continues on once we're dead and buried in the ground.

re·in·car·na·tion: the rebirth of a soul in a new body

Or perhaps, you are like most of the students and clients I work with and you find the idea of reincarnation fascinating, but aren't really sure it's true.

For me, the purpose of engaging with the notion of reincarnation is not to prove its existence, but instead to tap into its potential. Holding a view that this life is not the only life we've ever lived, or *will* ever live, can aid us in accelerating our present life healing process.

It can be difficult for some people to acknowledge that they're a soul in a human body because most of us will never know for certain that we have lived previous lives, or that a part of us will continue on after our present human body perishes.

In my opinion, this uncertainty doesn't matter because the pursuit of determining whether reincarnation is real or not will never bring us fulfillment. This type of needing to know is like scratching an itch that will never be relieved.

Instead of trying to figure out whether there is solid proof of past lives, I encourage you to simply be open to the idea that you might be a soul in a human body, even if you don't believe it completely. Approaching your own soul path with this type of open-minded curiosity will serve you well as you embark on a journey of learning to shift and heal your soul patterns (we get to soul patterns in the next chapter).

No matter what, one day we are going to die, and only then will we discover what actually happens when the body perishes. For now, we are here, we are alive, and we have things to do! What we do is of consequence, and we need to realize this in order to intentionally walk our soul path.

What we do really does matter!

And because what we do matters we need to get on with changing the way we habitually react to the events of our human life. Walking our soul path is not a future or a past activity. It is happening now. It is how we react to life in the present moment.

Reincarnation is the concept that some essence of our being, most often referred to as the soul, continues to live after this particular body dies.

We all need assistance in figuring out how to react to the present events in our life because the choices are so vast. In my opinion, people are generally committed to wanting to do a good job. Yes, some people have hate in their hearts, but most people don't. Most people want to make caring choices that will benefit both their own lives and the world as a whole.

But how do we know what the right decision is to do just that? When someone is rude to us we might wonder: Should I set a strong boundary with the person offending me? Or should I be forgiving and compassionate and just give them their space?

When we are scared of a new experience we might find ourselves unsure if we should push past our fear of trying something new or just accept that not every activity is for us.

These are just two examples of how it can be hard to know the best way to react to the situations life throws at us.

When we start to open up to the idea that we are a soul on a long journey, only temporarily inhabiting this human body, we can ask new questions to help us make the best decisions about how to react to our life situations. Questions such as: What soul lesson do I want to learn from this situation? Or how can I best be kind to my own soul throughout this challenge?

Pema Chödrön, Tibetan Buddhist Nun, and author of *When Things Fall Apart* explains:

> "I realize that whatever is happening to me is my karma ripening, and this is an opportunity to just be finished with it, have it burned up, have it transformed, like those seeds never have to come up again, because of the way I am working with what is happening to me now."

This is what walking the soul path entails: acknowledging that our choices matter, and that the soul patterns we create now will come with us into the future.

We will never know for sure what our soul has experienced before it inhabited our present body, but we can use the knowledge that we are a long-lasting soul to inform us in the decisions we make.

The goal of this book is not to convince you that past lives exist or that reincarnation is real, and the topic of reincarnation is bigger

than I am able to cover here.

But as we get further into how the energetic self healing process works, it can be helpful to be open to the concept of soul reincarnation. We don't only want to heal what we immediately know is bothering us. We want to heal *all* the soul pain we are experiencing, and that means healing the soul pain that was with us before we were born into this life.

You are a very important being, and this planet has a great need for your healing. All the soul pain you've accumulated on your long journey is innocent. Mistakes happen, that was true in the past and it is also true in the present. We are never going to avoid making mistakes, hurting ourselves or hurting others, but we can change how we react to these events.

We *can* move away from blame and feeling beaten down by suffering, and move towards committing to transforming everything that occurs on our soul path into energetic healing that our soul will take forward into the future.

19

20

Chapter Four

How Soul Patterns Are Created

Our main task while walking the soul path is to reverse and heal soul patterns that are no longer benefitting us.

To do this you need to understand that you are constantly being influenced by soul patterns created in your past lives. At the same time you are also creating new soul patterns through the choices you make each and every moment throughout this life.

kar·ma: the sum of a person's actions in this and previous states of existence, viewed as deciding their fate in future existences

Soul patterns are created through your behaviors, habits, and states of mind. Whatever activity you repeat becomes reinforced in your system eventually becoming an ingrained pattern in your life.

It is only when we're aware that our soul patterns are consistently informing our soul path that we're able to make lasting change to our life.

This is because patterns can be reversed. When we think that the way we are is just the way we are and nothing is ever going to

change, we become stuck and disempowered. Our healing potential is stifled.

When we realize that what we're experiencing is just patterning set through past choices, and that through making new choices we can create different patterns for our life, our healing potential becomes infinite.

Does this sound easy or hard to you?

Well, it is both.

Knowing that what has happened in our past does not need to inform our future is a belief we can embrace to make our energetic self healing incredibly profound and permanent. However, the actual letting go of the soul patterns can be hard, as we have come to falsely believe we are our soul patterns.

But we are not.

We are not our patterning.

We are long-lasting souls with free will, and we can make any soul path decision we want in this life. It takes courage to create new soul patterns, and I have no doubt you are a kick-ass warrior who has all the strength you need to change every soul pattern that no longer serves you.

All the choices you make are creating neural pathways in your

brain. The choices you make the most become the strongest neural pathways.

The neural pathways in your brain that have been traveled most frequently are now the easiest ones to travel.

> Walking the soul path means accepting that our problems might not be problems at all; but in actual fact are soul patterns we are capable of transforming.

Many of these neural pathways are beyond easy to travel. They have actually become automatic to travel. But just because a neural pathway is easy and automatic doesn't mean it is the one you *want* to be traveling. It really might not be the one best for you. To get the most benefit out of this incarnation we are presently living, we need to use the power of choice. Our soul patterns are not our fate, and they are not our identity or destiny.

Soul patterns are simply the easiest neural pathways for us to travel for the simple reason we have traveled them a lot.

Tara Brach, author and Buddhist teacher, explains it this way in her book *Radical Acceptance*:

> "The more we anxiously tell ourselves stories about how we might fail or what is wrong with us or with others, the more we deepen the grooves—

the neural pathways—that generate feelings of deficiency."

Our life does not feel good when the most used neural pathways we travel are a sense of inadequacy and deficiency. If we want to change our life we need to change these patterns by creating new neural pathways such as, self-acceptance and self-love, because these are the routes we *want* to be taking.

Neural pathways can be altered and soul patterns can be reversed. Change is possible and transformation of our lives and the planet as a whole is not only an option but is actually happening all the time. These exciting transformations begin with the awareness that there are habits and patterns we are choosing that we are not happy with. Once we see that change is needed we then need to be firm, yet kind, with ourselves about making different choices, even when it feels uncomfortable.

In the forest behind my house there is an intricate system of trails. This trail system has become altered in the time my family has been walking on them due to the choices we have made about which trails to take regularly.

Years ago, there was a wide main trail that we stopped using

because it didn't take us directly back to our house. We started a new little trail to bring us directly home. At first this new trail was

24

very difficult to find, but over time through use it has become the widest and most obvious trail, while what was once the main trail is now overgrown and hard to see.

This is happening all the time to our neural pathways. When we start a new pattern it is a tiny, little trail we can hardly find. But as we travel this new neural pathway more frequently it grows and eventually becomes the most obvious and easiest path to travel, while the old neural pathways we stop using, fades away.

Dr. Marsha Lucas tells us in her book, *Rewire Your Brain for Love*:

> "Remember, that experiences cause your neurons to fire, and that neurons that fire together wire together. In this way, the experiences you have shape your brain."

The most challenging part of altering our neural pathways is the beginning. It is awkward to start a new habit. We are bad at it at first. Truly, there is no grace in creating a new soul pattern. We just have to stumble through.

We have to remember that it will all be worth it. Over time as we travel neural pathway routes that we actually want to be part of our soul patterning, we become proud of what we are creating on our

soul path. Eventually these neural pathways that we are happy to be traveling are the routes that are also the easiest to travel. They can

even become the ones that are automatic for us to travel. Satisfactory healing on our soul path is possible.

Our soul pain is real, this is true. We all have neural pathways that are neurotic and even destructive presently wired into our system. This is part of the suffering we need to acknowledge on the soul path. A more significant truth, and the one we need to focus on now, is that we also have the ability to change these soul patterns and heal our soul pain effectively and permanently.

We just have to *do it!*

New neural pathways and healthy soul patterning are available to us. When we intentionally choose which pathways we are going to travel we will have succeeded at transforming our suffering into soul opportunity.

Chapter Five

<u>No Blame, No Shame When Transforming Our Soul Pain</u>

Transforming our soul patterns does not mean automatic happiness - and this is a good thing. If we were happy all the time, we would have no challenges to learn and grow from.

trans·form: make a thorough or dramatic change

Many of us are constantly forcing ourselves to feel happy, which often means we are avoiding our true feelings, and therefore strengthening soul patterning of self-denial. If we are overly focused on the positive and ignoring the negative, we are likely avoiding soul challenges that need our attention.

Admitting to our own unhappiness can be difficult because we have been taught that happiness is the optimal feeling.

We have been taught to 'always look for the positive' in every situation. The problem with engaging in fake positivity is that it is akin to applying a layer of candy coating of good thoughts over a gooey middle of pain. If you bite hard enough, the positive thinking will crumble and the real substance of suffering will inevitably be seen.

27

When we use positive thinking to avoid our pain because we don't like how it feels, we are repressing our pain and not actually healing it.

Thich Naht Han, Vietnamese Buddhist monk and peace activist explains:

> "The practice is to transform yourself. If you don't have garbage, you have nothing to use in order to make compost. And if you have no compost, you have nothing to nourish the flower in you. You need the suffering, the afflictions in you. Since they are organic, you know that you can transform them and make good use of them."

And we all have at least some garbage in our systems ready to be composted, but we can only do this effectively if we take sole responsibility for the pain we experience. Mostly we don't take responsibility for our own pain. Instead we blame others for our pain because we think it will hurt less than taking responsibility for it ourselves. In this way, we let our pain be the fault of our parents, our bosses, our spouses, the medical system, the government or society as a whole.

We believe that if one of these external sources would just change then we wouldn't have to feel so uncomfortable. But it is only

when we take full responsibility for our pain that we can transform it into something healing and of benefit to our soul path.

Taking responsibility is not the same as accusing ourselves. We need to be careful when we're taking responsibility for our own suffering that we are doing it from a place of self-love and empowerment, rather than turning the knife towards ourselves in anger and blame.

> Using our challenges as fuel for our healing builds confidence, opens our hearts and deepens our understanding of our own soul path.

We want to avoid taking a punitive approach to the healing process. We want to embody an attitude of loving-kindness when facing the pain within ourselves. By being willing to see that the pain and suffering we experience is ours and ours alone we can finally start doing something about it.

When you start to see that the pain you are experiencing is actually an inside job, do you get angry with yourself?

Many people do. Many people call themselves names such as: loser, screw-up, moron etc., when they realize that it is their own internal attitudes that are causing their own suffering.

But the transformation of our pain into soul path growth will never

materialize from treating our own self badly. Self-criticism is the way we become weaker and more fearful of the world. Self-blame and self-shaming has us believing that transforming our problems into something beneficial is an impossible task.

It isn't impossible at all. Actually it is totally possible.

The first step to healing soul patterns that aren't healthy for us is becoming aware of them. We need to know that when we see our neurosis clearly we are going to be able to use this information wisely and not as a weapon against ourselves.

Dr. Brené Brown, best-selling author of *Daring Greatly* explains:

> "Owning our story can be hard but not nearly as difficult as spending our lives running from it. Embracing our vulnerabilities is risky but not nearly as dangerous as giving up on love and belonging and joy—the experiences that make us the most vulnerable. Only when we are brave enough to explore the darkness will we discover the infinite power of our light."

This perspective that honestly acknowledging our own pain and suffering is the *only* path that will move us in the direction of healing is essential if we want to have the courage to turn our challenges into productive opportunities for transformation.

If there was another option we would all try to take it. There isn't. Facing our pain is the only option for healing our suffering.

No one really likes this. No one likes looking at their own darkness. It is frightening, it is lonely, and often we feel helpless and like we aren't strong enough to succeed. But these feelings pass.

Admitting that being aware and open to our pain is an incredibly difficult process helps us understand that we aren't failures in any way when we are finding life hard. We are just normal people doing a courageous thing.

It is only when we fully recognize that being human is intrinsically difficult that life actually becomes easier.

The Dalai Lama wisely tells us:

> "Every day, think as you wake up, today I am fortunate to be alive, I have a precious human life, I am not going to waste it. I am going to use all my energies to develop myself, to expand my heart out to others; to achieve enlightenment for the benefit of all beings."

We turn our problems into healing opportunities by working very consciously with our minds, our hearts, our bodies, and our energy. Instead of blaming ourselves when pain and trauma occur we can

realize that we have an opportunity in that moment of pain to create a new neural pathway- not because it is easy but because we love ourselves. Blame and shame will never bring us the healing we are looking for, only new choices towards the life we truly want will.

Chapter Six

Two Essential Questions

(or how to practice Mindfulness)

In any moment there are a million places we can put our attention.
Actually, there are way more than a million, the options are infinite.

mind·ful·ness: the quality or state of being conscious or aware of something

We can use our attention to think about hating people, to think about all the ways we have failed in our life, to feel hopeless, or to generate blame. We can also use our attention to feel the wind against our skin, watch a beautiful sunset, or feel empathy for a friend.

Our attention can go almost anywhere. This is a powerful realization because wherever our attention goes, that is the neural pathway being travelled. That is the soul pattern becoming rutted in. As you can imagine, it is important that we choose carefully where we place our attention, because these patterns are going to be with us for a long time on our soul path.

Do you really want all of your worrying, fretting and feeling sorry for yourself to be the neural pathway that is the easiest and most

automatic for you to travel? If you don't then you need to learn to steer your attention away from those thought habits. Just because you are thinking a thought, doesn't make it true. That thought is simply soul patterning that you can change and shift if you choose to.

Mostly though we don't feel like we have a choice about what we think. We feel like our mind is simply crazy, taking us on a wild goose chase to all types of destinations that we don't have any control over.

This belief that we have no control over our minds is extremely dangerous because our minds are not to be trusted. Our minds can easily go to dark and mean places, reinforcing old, dysfunctional neural pathways.

In his book, *The New Science of Personal Transformation*, Daniel Siegel explains:

> "One of the key practical lessons of modern neuroscience is that the power to direct our attention has within it the power to shape our brain's firing patterns, as well as the power to shape the architecture of the brain itself."

We become in control of our soul path and create beneficial wiring within us through becoming aware that we don't have to go on every insane roller coaster ride the mind tries to take us on. It's

actually very easy not to go wherever the mind tries to take us, all we have to do is use Mindfulness.

Purposely choosing where we place our attention is the most powerful thing we can do on our soul path and Mindfulness is the tool we train in to give us this ability. Mindfulness is extremely easy to learn and incredibly simple to practice. But it will only help us if we actually do it.

Jon Kabbat-Zinn, creator of the *Center for Mindfulness in Medicine*, explains:

> "Mindfulness means paying attention in a particular way: on purpose, in the present moment, and non-judgmentally."

Purposefully paying attention to the present moment is a skill we all need to learn. Much of the time we are living in the past or in the future through the direction our thoughts are taking us, but our actual life takes place in the present moment.

Mindfulness is the tool we use to train ourselves to intentionally choose where to place our attention.

When we don't pay attention to what is happening in the present moment we are literally missing out on our life. Paying attention to the present moment doesn't come naturally to us, though.

This is why we call Mindfulness a practice, because we need to practice it to become capable at it.

I sum up the skill of Mindfulness with the technique of asking ourselves two essential questions:

1. *Where is my attention now?*

2. *Where do I want my attention now?*

We can ask ourselves these two essential questions in any given situation.

Let's say that I am walking my dog and I want to practice Mindfulness on the walk, I will start with asking myself the first question; *where is my attention now?* And perhaps when I take a conscious look at my own attention I see that I'm thinking about a workshop I'm teaching the next day. Now that I know where my attention is I can ask the second question; *where do I want my attention now?*

If the answer to the second question is that I want to keep thinking about the workshop I'm teaching the following day, because I still have some details to work out then I just leave my attention where it is, feeling assured that I'm making a purposeful choice to think about the workshop.

But maybe the answer to the question; *where do I want my attention now?* is that I don't want my attention to be on planning the workshop because everything for the workshop is already prepared. Perhaps my notes are neatly on my desk at home ready for the

36

following day, and I'm doing nothing more than ruminating unnecessarily about a future scenario.

In this case, I would decide that thinking about the workshop is not where I want my attention and I would make the choice to shift my attention elsewhere. I will shift my attention to noticing my breath, or if I am in a beautiful area I might shift my attention to looking at the trees or other nature around me.

Having the knowledge that where I put my attention is a very powerful experience that is creating my soul patterns motivates me to choose carefully where I place my attention. This is the gift Mindfulness offers us; the power of conscious choice. In the following chapters we will talk more about beneficial places to bring our attention to.

For now what is important about the above example is that I don't spend any time criticizing or blaming myself for where my attention is. Instead I feel empowered by my ability to purposely shift my attention where I want it.

We can ask these two essential questions regularly as an informal Mindfulness practice, and employ Mindfulness in *any* situation: washing the dishes, drinking coffee, driving, going for a walk, having sex, talking with a friend, or falling asleep at night.

By using these two essential questions: *where is my attention now?* and *where do I want my attention now?* You will be ensuring that you're

making conscious choices about what neural pathways you are strengthening.

We can also use these two essential questions as part of a formal Mindfulness Meditation practice. With patience, willingness, and a little effort, anyone can practice Mindfulness Meditation.

Mindfulness Meditation is the process of sitting quietly for a set amount of time and moving our attention to a point of awareness (usually the breath) repeatedly. To some people the idea of practicing Mindfulness Meditation seems incredibly boring, or even impossible.

Is this you?

Have you tried Mindfulness Meditation before and immediately felt like a failure because you weren't able to quiet your mind?

Well, welcome to the club. Experiencing a loud mind when you try to meditate is not you being 'bad' at meditating. It is just a normal part of being human for the mind to be busy—even when we try to meditate.

Everyone who meditates sometimes (or more than sometimes) has the experience of feeling bothered by a loud and busy mind. This is what we can expect to happen when we meditate. Because the purpose of meditating is not to feel peaceful, become calm, or get good at meditating.

We practice Mindfulness Meditation so that we can train ourselves to kindly re-direct our attention. It is only when our mind is acting busy and crazy that we have the right conditions to practice this skill.

Seriously, we all have crazy minds, it's not just you. This is the whole reason we need to practice Mindfulness Meditation.

We don't want to worry or fret about the state of our crazy mind because we aren't trying to change or fix ourselves through Mindfulness. We aren't trying to turn into someone different or be somehow better. Instead, with Mindfulness Meditation, we are simply learning how to become more aware of ourselves exactly as we are.

As a Mindfulness Meditation instructor, I have had the honour of observing as many students shift from feeling overcome by emotional anxiety, due to the busyness of their brain, to a place where they feel like they have the ability to be in control of their own state of mind. This often occurs after practicing Mindfulness Meditation a few times a week for a month or so.

Mindfulness Meditation is awkward at first because the practice itself is forming a new neural pathway. As we practice Mindfulness Meditation regularly, it becomes more natural. People often end up really falling in love with how it feels to practice Mindfulness Meditation. They enjoy the results of being able to make

purposeful choices about how they want to react to both mundane and challenging situations.

Formal Mindfulness Meditation trains you to effectively shift your attention on command. If you truly want to be able to employ the skill of Mindfulness each and every day, you need to practice Formal Mindfulness Meditation at least a couple of times a week. This is the way you will become capable and experienced at choosing where to purposely put your attention.

The Formal Practice of Mindfulness Meditation

In the formal practice of Mindfulness Meditation, we use the breath at the nostrils as a focus point for training ourselves to become better at purposely shifting our attention. To practice Formal Mindfulness Meditation you need to find a quiet place you can sit comfortably with our eyes closed (or eyes open if you prefer), for a reasonable length of time.

Once you are sitting comfortably, you can use the two essential questions to help you continually return your attention to your breath every time your attention strays. Over and over again you will ask yourself silently in your mind; *where is my attention now?* and *where do I want my attention now?*

In the formal practice of Mindfulness Meditation, the answer to the question *where do I want my attention now?* is always the breath at the nostrils (or if that isn't appropriate, the breath at the belly).

In this way we are practicing moving our attention on command so that we can become capable of purposely choosing where to place our attention during any activity or situation.

Mindfulness Meditation Technique

Step #1. Sit comfortably on a pillow on the floor or in a comfortable chair (I discourage people from lying down because it can be difficult to stay alert).

Step #2. Move your attention to the breath at the nostrils and really feel the breath as you inhale and exhale. Try to ensure you aren't imagining the flow of breath in your mind, but that you're actually feeling the sensations of texture and movement inside of your nostrils as the breath moves in and out.

Step #3. Notice how your attention doesn't stay on the breath for long, but almost immediately jumps to a thought, a memory, a worry or a fantasy (or somewhere else). This is not you failing at the practice in any way. Your attention moving away from your breath is actually the most normal part of the practice.

Step #4. Ask yourself, *where is my attention now?* and then notice what has your attention. Don't engage with the thoughts that have your attention, just notice what is going on inside of you. Also, try to avoid having an opinion or judgement about what you are thinking about. Just gently notice where your attention is and then ask yourself; *where do I want my attention now?* The answer is always back at the breath at the nostrils, so shift your attention back to the breath at the nostrils.

Step #5. The entire Formal Mindfulness Meditation practice is repeating Steps #2 through #4 for as long as you choose to sit quietly and practice. I recommend 5 to 10 minutes (or longer if you wish).

This is the training process. There is nothing you are trying to achieve with this Formal Mindfulness Meditation practice other than learning the skill of moving your attention back to your breath.

There is nowhere that your attention can go that you won't be able to bring it back to the breath from. Every time you bring your attention back to the breath at the nostrils, you're strengthening your ability to purposely steer your attention.

Chapter Seven

From Mindfulness to Working With Energy

Once we understand that at any time we can choose where we want our attention to go, the next step is exploring all of the different places we can bring our attention to.

en·er·gy: the strength and vitality required for sustained physical or mental activity

One of these places is our personal energy.

Energy is experienced in a different way than our thoughts are. Whereas our thoughts are experienced in our mind, our energy is experienced through our senses.

We know we are touching into our energy when we feel subtle sensations, temperature changes, or movement inside our bodies and/or in the space around our bodies.

When we bring our attention to our energy we magnify the healing results on our soul path substantially, because our soul patterns, and the pain associated with our soul patterns, are stored within our personal energy. By purposely paying attention to our energy, and eventually learning how to clear and heal our energy, we can make substantial shifts towards health and well-being.

Barbara Ann Brennan explains to us in her book, *Hands of Light*:

> "Our physical bodies exist within a larger 'body,' a human energy field or aura, which is the vehicle through which we create our experience of reality, including health and illness. It is through this energy field that we have the power to heal ourselves."

We can think of the Universal energy field as a big web of interconnecting life force energy that connects everything. Each of us also has a personal energy field which connects in to the wider collective energy field.

Everything we do and everything we think impacts both our personal energy field and the collective energy field. This is how powerful each one of us is!

The secret power of the energy field is its capacity for storage. The energy field is essentially one big storage system for everything in the Universe. Information is constantly being added to our collective and personal energetic storage systems, and it can also be removed. When we stand in the power of this reality, and use it wisely, we can heal our lives in miraculous ways.

Our personal energy field holds all the information that makes up who we are: physically, emotionally, mentally, energetically, and spiritually. This information has been collected throughout our soul

journey's, which means there is information in our fields from our present and past lives, as well as from time spent in other realms.

This is one of the main reasons our present human journey is so confusing. There is more information in our personal energy field then we will ever fully understand, and what is so great about energetic self healing is that we really don't have to understand what all the information is.

Energetically healing ourselves does need us to analyze or even be cognizant of all the energy in us, or surrounding us. Energetic self healing just requires us to engage with our energy as it is, and to make purposeful decisions about how we want our energy to be aligned.

The realization that we have the ability to heal ourselves through paying attention to our own energy is a complete game changer on the human/soul path.

Have you ever felt or seen energy?

Maybe you clearly know that you've experienced energy. Or maybe you aren't so sure if what you felt one time was actually energy moving or changing. That is fine. Learning to experience energy is a practice just like Mindfulness.

The more you practice steering your attention to feeling, sensing and experiencing energy the stronger and clearer the sensations and experiences will become.

45

Many people relate naturally with energy in that they see and feel energy easily. For instance, they may see energy fields, which can also be referred to as auras. Seeing energy is called clairvoyance. Energy fields are often seen as white or green light (or other colors) hovering near and around the body. However, it is important to remember that the energy field is much more than light and colors-it is information.

Clairsentience is a term used for feeling or sensing energy, either in our bodies or in our minds but most often with our hands. In my opinion, everyone has the ability to experience clairsentience which is great because through accessing the skill of clairsentience information in the energy field can be changed.

Truthfully, our energy and everyone's energy is changing all the time anyways, but by becoming aware of how energy feels we can become intentional about working with the energy, so that *we* are the ones changing our energy in the direction we want our lives to go.

We are mostly accustomed to giving all of our attention to our thoughts and what the mind is doing. Because of this, we miss out on the experience our energy is having. When we become competent at Mindfulness we can choose to move our attention to our senses instead of our mind, and experience what our energy is doing within and around our body.

Being willing to pay attention to experiences beyond the mind is

46

how we access our energetic self healing potential because everything we need to heal is stored in our energy.

When we access our energy field storage, we can find soul patterning, soul pain, and where we are stuck on our soul path, and then take steps to clear and heal it. The ability to work purposely with our energy is a complete game-changer on the soul path, because instead of being a victim to our suffering, we can find the blockages the suffering has caused within our energy and change it.

The Connecting to Your Energy Self Healing Technique is an opportunity to practice feeling what your energy is like. This technique is a way to strengthen your neural wiring in the direction of being more aware of your energy.

Connecting to Your Energy Technique

Step #1. Come into a comfortable sitting or lying down position. Take a few mindful breaths by bringing your attention to fully feeling your inhalations and your exhalations.

Step #2. Bring all of your attention to your hands and really feel them. Feel the sensations under the skin. If your attention goes to a thought in your mind, bring it back to feeling and noticing the sensations in your hands.

Step #3. Keep noticing your hands. See if you can feel them becoming tingly, hot or cold.

Step #4. Continue to notice your hands and see how the sensations shift and move. Notice how every moment the sensations in your hands feel different. This is the energy moving.

Step #5. Bring your attention to any other body part you would like to feel the energy in. Try your feet, hips or stomach. Just notice how that body part feels under the skin and keep your attention there. Ensure you aren't thinking about the body part in your imagination, but actually bringing your attention to *feeling* the body part you are working with.

Step #6. Set your intention that you are noticing your energy field and bring your attention to the space around your body. What do you feel? The sensations you feel will probably be very subtle. If your attention shifts to your thoughts, just bring it back to the space around your body again. This takes practice. Stick with it and try it out a few times. Whenever you feel lost, bring your attention back to your hands and feel how the energy has shifted.

Step #7. Return to noticing your inhalations and exhalations of your breath. Congratulate yourself on experiencing your personal energy.

What Connecting To Your Energy Feels Like

Some of the common physical sensations people experience when they tune into their own energy are:

- tingling sensations under the skin

- experiencing temperature shifts of cold, warm, or hot

- experiencing twitching in various parts of the body

- feeling sleepy or lethargic

- feeling more energized

- feeling dizzy or foggy in the head

- stomach gurgling and/or burping

- aches or pains appearing and then quickly dissolving

Chapter Eight

It's All About Vibration

The term personal vibration can be misleading. When we imagine vibration we often conjure up an image of something moving, shaking and shifting, when in fact personal vibration simply refers to the way in which our personal energy communicates to the collective energy.

Our personal vibration isn't something we will ever see with our eyes or grasp with our minds. Instead when we become aware of our personal vibration we will *feel* it in our bodies.

vi·bra·tion: a person's emotional state, the atmosphere of a place, or the associations of an object, as communicated to and felt by others

I am sure you've actually already felt your personal vibration many times. When someone compliments you or tickles your back. When you have an orgasm or are involved in some type of other special moment and your whole body tingles and comes alive— that is you feeling your personal vibration.

Our personal vibration feels like tingling sensations under our skin, throughout our entire body. We can even feel the tingling sensation

51

of vibration in the space around our body, above our head, or next to our arms.

Sit still for a moment, right now, and notice what it feels like under your skin. Now feel the air around your body. Can you feel the subtle sense of movement? This is your vibration. This is your vibration broadcasting all of your personal energetic information to the Universe RIGHT NOW.

Our vibration is the critical link that connects our personal energetic information to the rest of the world. It is our vibration that tells the Universe what circumstances and experiences to give us, based on the information stored in our energy.

This can be a hard truth to accept. If you have an illness, have lost someone you love or are generally really struggling in your life, it may not feel comfortable to consider that it's your own energy causing these challenges. This perspective might even seem like victim-shaming.

It's not my intention to blame or shame anyone for anything. I want to be crystal clear that in no way is anyone *purposely* inviting problems or challenges into their lives with their vibration. That is not the way it works. People don't wake up in the morning and think; "I am going to cause myself difficulty with my own energy and vibration today."

Instead this process of our mind communicating with our energy, which in turn influences our vibration, is mostly unconscious and

unintentional. This is what we are looking to change on our soul path.

Our energetic information is very complicated due to our twisty, turny soul path. There is so much unconscious information stored in everybody's energy, and much of it is unhealthy. But just because we don't know about this energetic information in our systems, doesn't mean it isn't influencing our lives.

The unconscious soul path information that is stored in your energy is definitely influencing your life. All the time!

It is true for everyone that the information in their energy is the sole influence of the vibrational communication being broadcasted to the Universe. This means it is our energy that is informing what's happening to us. This is just the way it is. It isn't your fault, and it isn't my fault, it is just how things work. When we are brave enough to acknowledge that *everything* happening to us is soul opportunity being created by our own energy, we can start creating the fulfilling life of love and service we desire.

> Our personal vibration is how our energy communicates information to the Universe.

Using the knowledge that our personal energetic information is causing our life to be the way it is, for good or for bad, can motivate us to be purposeful and intentional about the vibration we are creating.

Esther Hicks, author of *Law of Attraction; The Teachings of Abraham* explains:

> "The Universe doesn't hear what you are saying. It
> feels the vibration you are offering."

What we put into our energy is what we get out. Some of our thoughts and intentions, both positive and negative, have been purposefully put in our energy. Some of them we are unconsciously creating. But everything we put into our energy is being communicated to the Universe all the time through vibration.

This is why we train in Mindfulness—so we can be more purposeful about how we are steering our attention. Wherever our attention goes is the information our energy hears and hence what our vibration communicates.

This does not mean we can never feel bad. This does not mean anytime we have a worry or feel sad our energy and vibration is getting messed up. Emotions themselves do not become dysfunctional information stored in our energy. It is our reactions to our emotions that are causing the energetic misalignment we need to heal.

Our soul path does not require us to always feel good and positive all the time. This would be an unauthentic way to live because we all have the ability to experience the full range of emotions. We need to use this ability. Having the full range of emotions won't hurt your vibration in any way.

Disappointment, grief, sadness, and anger are experiences that are important for our soul growth and they can be beneficial for us if we are being kind, loving, and open to a belief that healing is possible, even while we are hurting.

If we allow ourselves to hold kindness and acceptance in our hearts and minds, even while feeling bad, the this self-love will become the information our vibration is communicating to Universe, and will affect the nature of the circumstances we attract into our lives. Kindness and acceptance can become a way of life, but only if we make it so.

The biggest benefit of engaging in energetic self healing is that our vibration will improve. This is the main premise of energetic self healing. When we change what is inside of us, our external circumstances and the opportunities we attract into our life will also change. This happens because of the change to our vibration.

The Raise Your Personal Vibration Technique is quick to learn, efficient to use in any situation, and will only increase in strength and potency as you continue to engage with it.

Raise Your Personal Vibration Technique

Step #1. Come into a comfortable position, sitting, standing or lying down. Take a few mindful breaths by bringing your attention to fully feeling your inhalations and your exhalations.

Step #2. Now shift your attention to your hands. Really sense the energy in both of your hands. Feel the slight tingling sensation that starts to grow in your hands. Intentionally make the tingling sensation stronger by focusing on it.

Step #3. Use your attention to send the tingling sensations through your entire body. Very quickly let the tingling sensations travel up your arms and simultaneously down your torso and legs and up to your head, too.

Step #4. If you don't feel the energy move through your body on your first try, then try again. Just use your attention to nudge the energy up your arms and into the rest of your body. If your energy and vibration have been stuck for many years, it can take a few tries to get it moving again. Don't give up.

Step #5. Try this same exercise using your feet. Focus your attention on the feet until you feel the tingling sensations of vibration, and then use your awareness to send the sensations all the way up your body to your head and down your arms.

The more you do this technique of Raising Your Vibration, the stronger the tingling sensations will become. After some practice, you will be able to use this technique to Raise Your Vibration anytime and anywhere.

When Should You Raise Your Personal Vibration?

The technique of Raising Your Personal Vibration asks you to bring all of your attention to the sensory experience in your body. A raised vibration feels like your whole body is tingling and alive.

Sometimes it feels impossible to change our thoughts. A recurring thought of anger or resentment just won't stop no matter how hard we try to notice our breath or look at the pretty trees.

When we are feeling like we can't get out of a negative thought cycle one choice we can make is to simply turn our attention completely away from our thoughts and move it to the sensory awareness of raising our vibration.

This is a sure way to positively alter any situation you are in.

Chapter Nine

The Power of Intention

How we direct our thoughts influences our reality more than most of us are willing to acknowledge. When we are constantly thinking that things won't work out for us, we give that message to our energy.

This energetic information then becomes a vibrational communication, which is broadcasted to the Universe stating "Things won't work out." And then guess what? Things don't work out for us. "Oh, I just knew I wasn't going to get the job... win the raffle... have fun at the party last night," we might think to ourselves. But did you just know? Or is that the intention you, yourself, put into your energy and therefore what your vibration attracted to you? Remember what we put into our energy is what we get out.

in·ten·tion: an aim or plan

Wayne Dyer, spiritual teacher and author of *The Power of Intention* explains:

"Intention creates our reality."

Your energetic operating system is not static; it is incredibly dynamic. It is responding to everything you are thinking and doing,

ALL THE TIME. This is why it is important on your soul path to make intentional choices about what information your heart and mind is putting into your energy.

When we are purposeful with our intentions in a proactive way, we can effectively heal our soul patterns and create the life we really want.

People tend to focus on whether their thoughts and actions are 'right.' They want assurance that there is a way they can act, or be, that will ensure they won't have any more difficulties in their life. But this is impossible, because our actions can't be 'right' and they can't be 'wrong' from the perspective of energy and vibration. This is because your energy and vibration aren't responding to your actions; they are responding to your intentions.

This is a big concept to grasp because all too often we are focused on how we look physically or how we are perceived externally instead of paying attention to the real powerhouse of our existence which is what thoughts we are holding in our mind, and what intentions we are holding in our heart. We miss out on being cognizant of this crucial information because we are too caught up in worrying about what decisions are right and what decisions are wrong and what other people think of us. This causes us to lose sight of what our souls need.

> Everything we do with our hearts and minds is understood by our energy as intention.

What our soul needs is purposeful intentions that take us on the path we *want* to be walking on this soul journey. There is no fate, everything can change at any moment, and everything is changing in every moment. We need to ensure that it is our own selves who are directing that change. This is done by putting beneficial intentions into our energy.

It is a waste of our time to be constantly evaluating if a decision is the right or wrong one to make. There is no right or wrong; there is only intention. The goal of the soul path is to get more efficient with applying this reality.

If we are feeling confused about what we want to create on our soul path all we need to do is choose what outcome we want for our life and then hold that intention in our mind and heart and then just go ahead and *make* decisions. It is the intention creating the outcome, not the specific action.

If we want to feel more peaceful then we just state in our energy; 'I am feeling more peaceful" and then place this intention on any and every choice or action we make. If we want to have more love directed towards us we need to state in our energy; "I feel loved" and then move forward with *any* action knowing this is the intention implanted in that choice.

Our hearts and minds are powerful instruments of change. So, let's use them!

I learned a lesson about my heart and mind informing my own

energy the hard way a few years ago. I was in Toronto, riding the subway, when a man started talking to me in a friendly manner. I learned that the man was from Israel and that his son had just undergone a lung transplant. However, his credit card had expired before he could purchase the medicine he needed for his son, and he had just gone to the main credit card office to try to get the issue resolved, but they wouldn't help him. The man told me he was worried because he was traveling with his son back to Israel the following day and he didn't know how he would get the money to buy the medicine.

As the man was telling me his story, I was overcome by a wave of nurturing and loving energy. I felt like his son was my son, too, and suddenly money didn't seem to matter to me. All that mattered to me in that moment was that his son was healthy and safe. Without thinking twice, I heard myself telling the man I would get him the money he needed to buy the medicine for his son.

As I walked to the bank machine, this loving energy consumed me. I took out the cash from the machine and handed the money over to the man. I gave him my address so he could pay me back and walked away. After we parted, the feeling of love lingered in my system for about five minutes more. Then in a blink of an eye, it was gone, as I started to realize I had most likely been conned. The overwhelming love I had felt just a minute before has now completely switched to anger. Not anger against the man, but anger

at myself. Anger at my own stupidity. A hot shame filled my body and I cursed myself for being so naïve.

A week later, I called my friend who had been a Thai Forest monk for 17 years and told him this story. My friend told me something about intention that taught me how powerful our hearts and minds are. He said, "You made good karma when you gave the money, as your intention was good. But then you made bad karma with your negative thoughts towards yourself."

My friend reminded me that what is creating our karma, or our soul patterns, is not the action itself but the intention we are holding with our hearts and mind at the time of the action.

When I held love in my system for this man and his son, I was strengthening a soul pattern of generosity, compassion, service and love. But when I berated myself for being gullible and stupid I was strengthening a soul pattern of self-hate within myself that is a deep canyon I have traveled many times.

Really this man on the subway gave me a gift. He provided me with the opportunity to taste a type of Universal love that I knew I wanted to spend more time with.

We tend to beat ourselves up for things that happen that aren't really deserving of our criticism. Most of the time our heart means no harm; most of the time our intention is to help, not to hinder or

hurt anyone. Then why do we beat ourselves up over what we deem as bad choices, when really we are just trying to do our best?

When we beat ourselves up over perceived mistakes, we are sending the intention of self- hate and inevitably self-limitation into our energy, and then this is the vibration getting communicated to the world around us. If we keep doing this, we end up in a nasty cycle where we feel like negative things keep 'happening' to us. However, perhaps these negative things aren't just accidently happening to us. Perhaps we are getting the results of the information we are putting into our energy

Breaking out of this cycle of unconsciously putting misguided information into our energy is only possible if we stop letting our hearts and mind hold negative intentions towards ourselves.

We are never going to get this life right. There is no way to completely prevent making mistakes. This is out of our control. What is in our control is how we react to these mistakes and how we react to all of the circumstances life presents us with.

We *can* control how our mind is reacting and we *can* control how our heart is reacting. This is something we just need to learn how to do.

Pema Chödrön, Buddhist nun and teacher explains:

"War and peace start in the human heart. Whether that heart is open or whether that heart is closed has global implications."

Intention is the most important skill we use when engaging in energetic self healing. Energetic self healing is possible because we set the intention in our energy that it *is* possible.

This is how powerful we each are. We each can decide what is possible through the thoughts we think. At first we might feel skeptical about having this amount of power, but as we start to become increasingly aware that our intentions are becoming our reality, we realize that purposeful intention setting is our true superpower. When we use intention to benefit our soul path, our healing is profound, and the people we love benefit, too.

Being Playful with Intentions

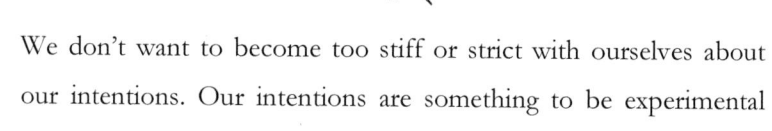

We don't want to become too stiff or strict with ourselves about our intentions. Our intentions are something to be experimental and creative with, because learning how to skillfully work with intention is a process of trial and error. So just play with it.

Each day you can set an intention for your day and then just observe what happens. Through this process of purposely engaging

in intention setting you will deepen your understanding of how intentions become your personal energetic soul programming, influencing your vibrational communication with the Universe.

The intentions you set with your mind and heart for the day should be stated in the present, optimistically and with an open heart without a need for a very specific outcome.

Some examples could be:

- Today I am feeling appreciated for my contributions.
- Today I feel ease in all my activities.
- Today a new opportunity comes my way.
- Today I feel connected and supported by others.

Right when you wake up in the morning think one of these intentions or choose one of your own. Think it in your mind, and feel it in your heart. Do this for a minute or two and then gently observe what happens over the course of your day. Again, we aren't trying to get this right—we are just being playful. We are just having an experience and learning more about how intentions affect our energy, vibration, and the circumstances of our life.

Chapter Ten

Guidance for Working with Your Energy

There is no right or wrong way to work with our energy. No one is going to give you a gold star if you work with your energy right, and no one is going to give you a time-out if you work with your energy wrong.

We need to let go of our desire to evaluate our energetic self healing experience as a good or bad, and just *have* an experience.

> There is no way to fail at energetic self healing. Feeling good is not a sign of success and feeling bad is not a sign of failure.

Of course, it's normal to feel tentative about trying something new, especially something as important as healing your energy. You might even be wondering, "What if I twist my energy in the wrong direction and things turn out worse than they are now?"

I am here to tell you that this isn't possible. The healing that happens in energetic self healing doesn't come from moving the energy in any direction. The healing happens through the intention of love and wellness we hold for ourselves.

Remember, it is the intention we are holding that creates the reality

of the healing experience and we don't need to get too technical about how to set the intention properly. All you need to know is that the moment you connect to your energy for the purpose of healing, you are innately holding a loving intention towards yourself.

When we go into our energetic healing practice knowing that health and well-being is the natural intention of energetic self healing we can let go of any fear of hurting our energy.

The goal of these energetic self healing techniques is not to make you believe in energy, see energy, or convince you of anything at all. The point of practicing these energetic self healing techniques is to learn manageable tools and techniques to help you feel more empowered to create the life you want.

When you become confident in your ability to use energetic self healing techniques you will begin to see yourself as capable of changing the information stored in your energy. This is what working with our energy offers us: the chance to be empowered to transform our challenges into opportunity.

Many people struggle to connect with their own energy because they aren't sure what they are experiencing is real.

Our energy is a mystery. We will never know for sure what is real and what is not. We just set the intention for healing, and for our

highest good, and let go of any attachment to knowing what is definitely real when connecting with our energy.

We don't worry about whether what we're experiencing is the exact truth when practicing energetic self healing. Instead we keep our minds open to whatever we experience while allowing our heart to be full of self-love.

When working with our energy, it is also important to let go of our attachment to wanting immediate results. When we are deeply attached to an outcome of wanting to feel good immediately, or if we are desperate for our problems to magically disappear, the intention we are sending to our energy is one of desperation and urgency. This type of intention has a repelling effect in our energy, causing our vibration to push away our healing potential.

When engaging in energetic self healing we need to relax and adopt attitudes of patience, willingness, self-love, and curiosity. We will never know all the details of what our soul needs to develop in this lifetime, so we don't know what challenges are going to be helpful to us on our soul path; this is why we can't micro-manage our healing.

Working with your energy is not like doing a carpentry job. There are no exact measurements or pre-conceived outcomes. When you connect with your energy, you're stepping into the mystery of your eternal soul path. The most profound healing experiences occur

when we are willing to explore this mystery fully without judgement, blame or attachment to outcome.

Our intentions for energetic self healing are most effective when they are broad and not too specific. When we become open, willing and available to health, love, kindness, possibility and support, we become available for healing experiences even though we don't know exactly how they will occur. We do know they'll only be able to occur if we are treating ourselves well.

Being mean to ourselves when we don't like the way we are feeling is never beneficial for our energy.

Sally Kempton, author of the book *Meditation for the Love of It*, explains:

> "This much should be obvious: you can't deal with thoughts by taking them out and shooting them. The delicate, intelligent energy we call the "mind" does not respond well to harshness."

Our thoughts don't like harshness, and neither does our energy.

When I do private energy healing sessions, I often see that people's energy has been damaged by how they have been treating themselves. We are all way too hard on ourselves, and this cruel self-criticism causes energy leaks, energetic congestion and

blockages in the chakras (we'll talk more about the chakras in Chapter 14).

And without even seeing your energy I can tell you the same is probably true for you. You're most likely damaging your energy with the mean thoughts you are thinking about yourself, and the sooner this stops the healthier your energy will be.

The point is we don't want our energetic self healing practice to become just another place we are doing damage to our energy by telling ourselves we are doing a 'bad' job. It would be totally counter-productive to hurt our energy in the process of trying to heal our energy by being overly critical throughout the process.

To avoid this happening you need to ensure you aren't pushing or pulling on your energy, or being too aggressive with yourself when doing your energetic self healing practice.

Energetic self healing isn't about you forcing your energy to change. It's about being open and available to the infinite healing that is available to you.

When we work with energy, we engage in a relationship with it. You can think of working with your energy as a kind of dance. Through every movement, you need to listen to what the energy is telling you, and then follow it as it shows you what needs to be healed.

Using the Energetic Self Healing Techniques

The energetic self healing techniques presented in this book are meant to be used in conjunction with your other health care routines. Please never use energetic self healing as a replacement for consulting your physician or other health care providers. Using conventional medicine alongside energetic self healing is the way forward for our collective increased healing results. Medical solutions to our ailments are vibrational manifestations. When we set the intention for healing we don't care what route brings the result of us feeling better. If we are prescribed certain drugs or surgeries that are going to benefit our life, then this could be the result of a positive vibrational communication between our energy and the Universe.

Also, please remember that the instructions in this book are just guidelines. We aren't trying to get working with our energy 'right', we are just having an experience. It's important that you do all of the energetic self healing techniques presented in this book in your own way. You are the expert on your life and your energy, so feel free to play and explore. Use my suggestions on how to do these techniques as a jumping off point and then listen and respond to what your energy is telling you. The more you show your energy you are willing to listen to it, the more it will talk to you.

72

Chapter Eleven

General All Purpose Energy Clearing

All of the information we have discussed in this book up to this point has been leading to this moment; learning how to energetically heal ourselves.

heal·ing: the process of becoming sound or healthy again

Energetic self healing is an incredibly stimulating, engaging, and visceral experience. And it isn't something we think about. It is something we *do*.

So, let's get going with it.

The General All Purpose Clearing Technique I am about to share with you asks of us to set a broad intention in order to clear all the information in our energy that isn't serving us. This technique can be done sitting in a meditation position, while going for a walk in nature, chilling out on the couch, or even simply lying in bed. It's important that you find a place you feel comfortable, relaxed, and able to feel open and willing to engage in the process.

The length of time you do this technique for is your choice. Sometimes 5 minutes is all we have time or energy for and sometimes we really want to take 30 minutes to an hour to do a full energetic clearing on ourselves. Don't get too hung up on where you do the technique or for how long. Just get on with doing it.

The General All Purpose Energy Clearing Technique uses the broad intention, *"All energies that are not serving my highest good are clearing from my system"* as a tool to clear all the trauma, pain, and faulty soul patterning you don't want to bring forth with you on your soul path.

What makes this technique so effective is the fact that the intention is very broad and overarching. The intention in this technique, when used willingly and wholeheartedly, allows the release of all old energies that are ready to be set free.

<u>General All Purpose Energy Clearing Technique</u>

Step #1. Come into a comfortable sitting or lying down position. Take a few mindful breaths by bringing your attention to fully feeling your inhalations and your exhalations.

Step #2. When you are ready, state the intention to yourself either out loud, or inside of your mind.

"All energies that are not serving my highest good are clearing from my system."

Step #3. Keep breathing and notice what you feel. If some parts of your body feel like they need to move, let them move. If you see or feel energy shifting, observe it with a loving attitude.

Step #4. If you don't feel or notice anything repeat Step #2. Sometimes it can take a few attempts at setting the intention for the energy to get moving. Trust whatever responses your body or energy makes and stay responsive.

Step #5. Stay with the energy as it moves and shifts for as long as feels comfortable.

Step #6. When it feels like the energy clearing has come to a natural end, return your attention to your breath.

Step #7. Notice how you feel in your mind, body, heart and energy.

Why This Technique Works

Using a broad intention deepens our healing because we let go of a need to 'know' what every pain or energetic block is, and instead just get down to healing whatever pain is there. When doing the General All Purpose Energy Clearing Technique we don't want to judge or analyze the energies that are leaving. Since we want to detach from these energies that are no longer serving us, we want to ensure we aren't giving them our attention.

Chapter Twelve
Intention-Setting Visualization Techniques

At this point you now understand that energetic self healing is not something we just read or talk about. It is something we *do*.

Engaging our imagination through the tool of visualization is one of the main ways we *do* energetic self healing.

vis·u·al·i·za·tion: the formation of a mental images

As children we were often encouraged to stop imagining so much. We may have been told to stop daydreaming or that by being in our imaginations we were too dreamy or unrealistic.

Visualization is using our imagination to strengthen our intentions in the direction of the life and soul path we want to be creating.

But we were born with the gift of imagination and this is fantastic because it is really beneficial and healthy for us to engage with our imagination. We can even use our imagination to heal ourselves.

Shakti Gawain, author of the book *Creative Visualization* explains:

"In order to heal themselves, people must recognize, first, that they have an inner guidance deep within and, second, that they can trust it."

The General All Purpose Energy Clearing Technique can become even more effective when you add visualization tools to it.

Strengthening the General All Purpose Energy Clearing Technique

Step #1. Set aside 10-30 minutes. Find a quiet spot where you won't be disturbed.

Step #2. Come into a comfortable sitting or lying down position. Take a few mindful breaths by bringing your attention to fully feeling your inhalations and your exhalations.

Step #3. Use your imagination to visualize your energy field. There are many ways you might see your energy field in your imagination. A common way to visualize the energy field is to see an image of your human body, and the space around your body as color or light. See if you can picture this image in your mind's eye. If another image comes up that feels like the energy field to you that is just perfect.

If you feel like you aren't able to visualize your energy field then you can use intention to get an image to come to you. State in your mind, *"I am visualizing my body and energy field."* Now notice what you see. (You can also always google 'energy field' and take a look at some images to help you get inspired.)

It doesn't matter what image you use to represent the energy field, just set the intention that you are visualizing an image or color, or feeling a sensation, that represents the energy field and this is what you can use for the clearing technique.

Step #4. Once you have a clear image of your energy field in your mind it is time to set the energy healing intention. State out loud or silently in your mind the words:

"All energies that are not serving my highest good are clearing from my system."

To strengthen this General All Purpose Energy Clearing Technique you can choose to get more specific about what energies you want to clear. This is your chance if you know there are a certain energies you want to clear from your system to do so.

Some examples of specific clearing statements are:

> *"All energies associated with my old job are clearing from my system."*
>
> *"All anger towards my ex-spouse is clearing from my system."*
>
> *"All the pain in my left knee is clearing from my system."*

Choose the wording that feels appropriate for you. Keep the wording optimistic and in the present moment.

Step #5. Use one of the following visualizations to help strengthen the intention and to intensify the clearing of old energetic information.

Clear the Darkness—Visualize darkness, blocks, or congestion clearing from your energy field. Imagine the energies that no longer serve your highest good as dirty, dark black, or gray energy flying out and off of your body and energy field and going all the way out the (real or imaginary) window. See the energy turn back into air or neutral energy. Keep going until no more dark, dirty energy is coming out of you.

Set Your Intention— Set your intention for the type of clearing you want to have happen, and then just stay with the sensations in the body, following the energy as it moves. Your intention might be; "any connections with the past are clearing" or "any hopelessness and self-hate is clearing." A good one we all need is, "all of my stress is clearing."

Then, hold an attitude of love and acceptance as you notice what you feel in your body as the energy moves and clears. If the energy moving slows down or stops altogether just re-state your energy clearing intention (Step #3) as many times as you need to. Keep bringing awareness to any sensations you experience in the body. It

80

is not uncommon to feel twitching, shaking, cramping, a need to stretch, or other sensations with this process.

If your eyes are closed, you might also see images behind your eyes. Don't become attached to any of the symptoms you experience in this process. Just keep following the sensations of the energy clearing with your awareness.

Do a Body Scan—Bring your attention to each part of your body from your feet to the top of your head, stating the intention in your mind's eye *"All energies that are not serving my highest good are clearing from my system."* As you get to each body part imagine darkness, or congested energy, clearing out of your energy field and body. Watch as the old energies float out the (real or imaginary) window and return to a clear, neutral state.

Step #6. When you feel like the clearing is complete, relax fully and return your attention to your breath.

Step #7. Take a moment to notice how your body, mind, heart, and energy feel.

Clearing Energy Is Not Always a Graceful Process

Clearing energy can also be understood as a type of spiritual surgery. Our energetic information is not only stored in our energy field but also in our body. When old energy is moved out, our body has to adjust to these energetic shifts in our system. This could result in any of the following symptoms:

- more frequent urination or bowel movements

- body twitches

- crying

- vomiting

- burping

- farting

- feeling more exhausted than usual

- feeling more energized than usual

As long as we are using the intention *"All energies that are not serving my highest good are clearing from my system,"* we know that any symptoms or reactions we experience are taking us in the right

direction on our soul path. However, whenever we have physical symptoms that concern us we should definitely consult a medical professional.

The point of energetic self healing though isn't to find immediate relief for what is ailing us, but is instead to heal the deep ingrained soul patterning we don't want to continue to be an influencing force on our soul journey.

Chapter Thirteen

<u>Strengthening Our Column of Light</u>

There is only one person on this planet that we spend all our time with; and that person is our self.

No amount of energetic self healing is going to provide lasting results on our soul path if we aren't committed to strengthening our internal column of light, and the way this is done is by committing to unconditional self-love.

> Our internal, energetic column of light is what our soul takes with us when we die.

Ask yourself honestly; "Would I spend time with myself if I had the choice?" This is a deeply personal and important question, and it's normal for the answer to feel uncomfortable.

Just take a moment now and consider how you treat yourself when your day isn't unfolding as you wish it would. Are you kind and patient with yourself? Do you say; "Oh well, we all have bad days sometimes." Or do you berate yourself for having had a terrible day by listing all the ways you should have done things differently?

It is extremely important that we are aware of how we are treating

ourselves because it has a big impact on our energy and on our soul development.

For now and into eternity we are all blessed with the opportunity to spend all of our time with our own soul. This is why we need to be good company for ourselves.

It's also true that when we're being cruel and impatient with ourselves, even if only in our minds, we are damaging our energy.

This is why energetic self healing is really a two stage process. Firstly, we need to clear out all of the old energetic damage that has occurred in our system due to the pain and trauma we have been exposed to in this life and in past lives. And secondly, we have to ensure we aren't inflicting new pain and trauma to our energy. We do this by being kind to ourselves no matter our circumstances.

Moving in the direction of kindness to ourselves is the journey of developing inner strength. Our internal column of light is the energetic representation of our inner strength. This is why we have incarnated: to develop inner strength and heal our internal column of light. This development in our inner column of light is what we take forward with us when we die.

We develop inner strength when we go through challenges and maintain unconditional love to ourselves even when life is rough. Being able to love ourselves even while everything is going really badly, is how we increase our belief in our self.

The most amazing skill we develop on the soul path is the belief that we can count on ourselves. This self-belief is stored in our internal column of light. We connect with our inner strength energetically through visualizing this column light within our own being.

What we want to create on our soul path is an internal column of light that is bright, strong, and bursting with vibrancy. This can only occur if we take the time to heal the old darkness, and ensure we aren't adding too much new darkness, as we go through the normal ups and downs of being human.

Connecting with our internal column of light allows us to find a non-intellectual way to heal our own sense of inadequacy.

Our clothes, money, homes, and even some of our relationships are impermanent, but our light is with us forever.

What Type of Light Do You Want to Have?

What type of light do you want to carry with you when you die? Do you want it to be dim and barely able to light up a room? Or do you want it to be bright, touching as many people as possible? If you want your internal column of light to be vibrant then you, yourself, will need to make it so.

Healing Your Column of Light Technique

Step #1. Come into a comfortable sitting, standing, or lying down position. Take a few mindful breaths by bringing your attention to fully feeling your inhalations and your exhalations.

Step #2. Next imagine a column of light coming from the center of the earth, up between your legs, through your tailbone, up your whole torso, through your neck and head, and out the top of your head, all the way up to space.

Step #3. Observe your column of light and get to know it. Notice that some places in your light column are wide and some are skinny. Notice that some places on the light column are bright and shiny and some are dull. Notice where there is darkness and even rips or tears in the light column. Don't judge any of it, just notice.

Step #4. Then choose your own creative way to work with visualizing your column of light. You want to see it becoming lighter and more vibrant. You can find your own way to do this or use one of the options below.

Awareness and Love to Increase Your Light— For this healing technique you don't want to push or pull on the light column or try to force it to change. Simply increase the strength of the light in the column by holding your attention on the light and sending it loving awareness. Keep watching the light and focus on feeling love towards yourself. Watch the light grow and shift, and let go of any need to 'do' anything. This simple loving awareness will brighten and strengthen your internal column of light every time.

No More Darkness— Visualize your light column and set the intention that any darkness you no longer need for your highest good in your light column is clearing. Visualize the darkness as smoke or congested energy leaving the light column, flying out the (real or imaginary) window and becoming clear energy. Use the intention; *"Any energies no longer needed for my highest good in my internal column of light are clearing."* Keep clearing the darkness until the light

89

column feels clear. This will probably need to be done multiple times.

Repairing the Tears— Another way the light column can be damaged is with small tears or rips where pain or trauma has left an energy leak in your light column. When you have energy leaking from your light column, it is difficult to feel completely energized. Imagine little pieces of your light traveling back to you and filling your inner being. When all of your light has returned to your light column, you can travel with your mind's eye up and down your light column, patching any tears with more light. Notice what happens in your body as you feel the light column becoming whole.

Step #5. When you feel like the energy healing in your light column is complete (or good enough for now) relax and bring your attention back to your breath.

Step #6. Take a moment to notice how you feel in your body, mind, heart, and energy.

Chapter Fourteen

Our Data Centers: The Chakras

Our personal and collective energy systems are more complicated, profound, and mysterious than we will ever fully understand.

Learning about our energetic systems is a journey we will travel for as long as our soul carries on, so there is no need to feel like we need to understand everything about how our energy works before we can start engaging with it for self healing purposes.

When we have the internal support of aligned chakra energy, our lives are more flowing and what we want manifests with ease.

There is, however, some information about the different components of our energetic system that are very easy to grasp, and can assist us on our soul path.

The chakras are a vital part of our energetic system. They are powerful data centers that exist within and beyond our bodies. The chakras are a vortex of vibration that store and communicate information about our entire soul path with the Universe.

Our chakras are the great manifesting agents of our life. They move

vibrational data in and out of our existence. Being informed about the chakras is incredibly useful information for us to have on our soul path. When we understand that it is in fact our chakras influencing our destiny, we can be wise in how we engage with our chakras. By connecting intentionally with our chakras for the purpose of healing we can clear out faulty data of our soul patterning and re-program the chakras with the information we want to be informing our lives.

Energetic self healing through the chakras is one of the most efficient and accessible ways to tap into soul path healing.

In her book *Intuitive Self Healing*, Marie Manuchehri explains the chakras further:

> "Each chakra has its own color and unique role in maintaining vitality in your body, mind, and spirit. Chakras are multi-dimensional, appearing round or cone-shaped. They form the main centers of a system that contains thousands of smaller energy points. The term chakra is a Sanskrit word meaning wheel or disk. Descriptions of the chakras first appeared in the Vedas, ancient spiritual texts dating back to 2000BC. This complex circuitry holds within it the keys to our evolution and wholeness."

In every moment the chakras are channeling information in and out of our systems. If the chakras are blocked with congestion, pain, or trauma, they become unable to channel information or data effectively, causing our energy to feel low, and our life to feel stuck. This is something we can easily change!

Exploring how the chakra system works can be quite exciting because it can deepen our understanding of what is happening in our own soul journey.

Each of the seven chakras governs a different area of our experience. When a major chakra is functioning optimally then the parts of our lives that the major chakra governs will also operate optimally.

The chakras are dynamic, which means they are constantly responding to our experiences, thoughts, and feelings. This is why working with our chakras through energetic self healing techniques can't just be done once, but needs to be a part of a regular energetic self-care practice.

The following chapters provide information about the major seven chakras and how to work with each one of them for soul path healing.

Chapter Fifteen

<u>Root Chakra</u>

The Root Chakra is our first chakra and is located centrally in the energy field just below the pelvis. The Root Chakra is responsible for our basic survival needs.

If you are having challenges with not feeling physically safe such as:

- having trouble maintaining housing
- worrying constantly about finances
- feeling like you don't deserve to have a good life
- having health issues that make you worry you won't survive
- being bullied or having your safety threatened
- feeling very indecisive about career or life choices in general

Then these can be signs that there is blockage or soul pattern damage to your Root Chakra. This is important to be aware of because the Root Chakra is fundamental for our soul healing. If we don't believe we are safe in the world, we easily go into a triggered state of feeling as if our very survival is being threatened. When

this type of fear or terror is triggered on a regular basis it is almost impossible to stay focused on more substantial soul path goals.

It is only when our energetic alignment is one of safety in the Root Chakra that we are able to make the courageous choice to be aware of our dysfunctional soul patterning and heal and reverse it.

The Root Chakra governs our basic survival need to feel safe in the world.

When we feel safe in our body and in our mind, it is a sign of healthy functioning in our Root Chakra. When the alignment in our Root Chakra is one of safety, we will be comfortable taking greater emotional and spiritual risks to move our life in the direction of soul fulfillment.

Healing of the Root Chakra can't be accessed with the mind. We need to heal the congested blockages where they exist, in the energy.

The Root Chakra Healing Technique will help you clear out any old, stagnant, energy in the Root Chakra that no longer serves you. This will increase the vitality of your Root Chakra, creating greater stability and confidence in your own existence.

Root Chakra Healing Technique

Step #1. Come into a comfortable sitting or lying down position. Take a few mindful breaths by bringing your attention to fully feeling your inhalations and your exhalations.

Step #2. Move your attention to the area just below your pelvis and visualize a red ball of light.

Step #3. Notice if there are any dark cords connected to the red ball of light. If there are dark cords then imagine all the cords being severed and dissolving away. This is different for everyone. You might have no cords, just a few cords or more cords then you can work with in one sitting. Just use visualization to clear as many cords as feels possible for you.

Step #4. Bring your attention to the red ball of light and set the intention for it to become brighter and stronger. You can also set the intention that; *"Any energies not serving my highest good in the Root Chakra are clearing."* Then see all the dark energy in the red ball of light clearing by going out the (real or imaginary) window and transforming into neutral, clear energy.

Step #5. Next, when you are ready, state the words in your mind's eye *"I am safe"* and send these words into the red ball of light. You can see the actual words in the red ball of light or just set the intention that the words *"I am safe"* are going into your Root Chakra. The specific technique you use is not as important as the strength of the intention.

Step #6. Repeat Steps #3 to #5 a few times in sequence.

Step #7. When you feel complete with the technique, return your attention to your breath and notice how your body, mind, heart, and energy feel.

What to Do If a Healing Crisis Occurs

If you have had a lot of trauma in your life that prevents you from feeling safe in the world, or have had a near death experience, there can be a significant amount of stagnation in the Root Chakra. If this is the case for you then this technique may need to be repeated on several occasions in order for you to be able to complete all of the steps and/or to observe any noticeable difference in your life.

It can also be possible that working intensely with Root Chakra healing can cause a 'healing crisis'. A 'healing crisis' is when your

symptoms become worsened instead of better as you engage in intentionally healing yourself.

A healing crisis is a sign that you need to be very compassionate with yourself. It is a sign that you are being very brave and courageous and the healing you are doing is deep and profound.

If you find your physical, emotional, mental, or spiritual symptoms worsening after engaging in the Root Chakra Healing Technique ensure you drink enough water to keep your system clearing effectively, get extra rest (even take time off work to avoid burnout if necessary), and reach out for help from trusted friends and health care professionals. No one needs to heal alone!

Chapter Sixteen

Sacral Chakra

The Sacral Chakra, our second chakra, is what I like to call our pleasure center. Located centrally in the energy field just below the belly button, this chakra is responsible for our creativity and sexuality, both of which are sacred and essential on our soul path.

We need pleasure in our lives. The soul path can be an upward climb, but it can also be full of fun and joy. This is what the Sacral Chakra asks of us to discover on our journey.

If the Root Chakra is all about 'I am alive' then the Sacral Chakra is all about 'I want to be alive'. This is a crucial belief system to hold if we are going to be motivated to heal ourselves, because not only do we deserve to feel safe on our soul path, we also deserve to experience joy as we travel our soul path.

Accepting that enjoying our life is important can be difficult for many people because somehow making money, being attractive, or not failing at our careers have become more important to many of us then enjoying the experience of being alive.

It can be hard to figure out what brings us enjoyment beyond the

superficial because of the soul patterning challenges we're all dealing with.

Much of what we call enjoyment is actually just the easy, automatic, soul patterning we actually need to transform. Often instead of being brave and looking for ways to bring ourselves real fulfillment on our soul path we use small pleasures of avoidance such as eating a piece of chocolate, drinking an alcoholic beverage, or watching one more TV show to distract ourselves. That little bit of sensory enjoyment pushes our true soul path goals of joy, creativity and pleasure deeper into the subconscious and causes the Sacral Chakra to stagnate.

This is how we become addicted to empty pleasures that don't bring us the satisfaction we are looking for.

If we continually deny ourselves pleasure and joy, we will never be in optimal alignment with our soul path. When we deny ourselves the sacred enjoyment of life, we lower our personal vibration which attracts unwanted circumstances.

As we heal the Sacral Chakra, we may find ourselves:

- experiencing more enjoyment in the process of creative activities (versus just being rushed to be finished)
- having more satisfying orgasms (through partnered sex or with ourselves)

- wanting deeper connections and stepping away from shallow relationships
- being less willing to go to a job or other activities that we don't enjoy or that are draining
- experiencing a deep gratitude for nature and places of beauty

The Sacral Chakra Healing Technique uses the tools of awareness and intention to strengthen the flow in the Sacral Chakra and shift the vibrational information being manifested to the Universe towards one of fun, pleasure, creativity and enjoyment.

Trigger Warning

If you have a history of sexual trauma this technique may bring up issues that you weren't aware were stored in your energetic system.

Even if you have thoroughly worked on healing old sexual trauma and feel like you are 'over it' your energy might tell you something different. This is not a sign of failure on your part, this is simply an opportunity to keep going on your soul path and deepen your healing process even more.

If after engaging with the Sacral Chakra Healing Technique you feel like traumatic issues have surfaced that need to be resolved, don't hesitate to reach out for support from a trusted friend or health care professional.

Sacral Chakra Healing Technique

Step #1. Come into a comfortable sitting or lying down position. Take a few mindful breaths by bringing your attention to fully feeling your inhalations and your exhalations.

Step #2. Bring your attention to your stomach or area around your belly button and notice if it feels stressed or relaxed.

Step #3. If your stomach feels stressed, purposely relax your stomach muscles to release the tension with a few slow, deep, belly breaths.

Step #4. Set the intention that all the stressful worries in your stomach are dropping into the earth to be composted. See the dark chunks of stress falling out and away from your body into the center of the earth.

Step #5. Next use your imagination to see your stomach filling with orange light. Watch the orange light as it travels into your stomach and becomes brighter and stronger.

Step #6. When the orange light feels bright, set the intention in your mind: *"I am open and available for pleasure."* Send these words into the orange light in your stomach.

Step #7. Watch the orange light and give it your loving awareness without judgement. Don't try to move the energy. If the tension returns to your stomach, don't judge or criticize, as this type of resistance is a normal part of the energetic self healing process. Just go back to step #3, release the tension again, and continue through steps #4 to #6 as many times as feels necessary.

Step #8. When you feel complete with the technique return your attention to your breath. Notice how your body, mind, heart and energy feel.

Chapter Seventeen

Solar Plexus Chakra

The third chakra, the Solar Plexus Chakra, is centrally located in the energy field just below the rib cage. The Solar Plexus Chakra is the data center for our self-esteem and self-worth. It is also our personal power center.

> When the Solar Plexus Chakra is functioning optimally it is easy to stand in our personal power.

Our personal power is very important to our soul development. We incarnate into human form to develop confidence in sharing our personal power with the world.

Carolyn Myss, author of *Anatomy of Spirit* and mystical teacher, tells us:

> "The reason you have descended into physical life
> is to unleash the power of your soul upon Earth."

By power Myss means our sense of authority, and autonomy, over our decisions, and our ability to act from our authentic value systems, even if they clash with the beliefs of others around us.

When Myss states that our purpose of incarnating is to 'unleash our

personal power' she also means that we need to share our natural gifts and talents with the world.

When the Solar Plexus Chakra is aligned we feel a natural sense of self-love and sharing our true self with the world is easy and natural.

When we exert our personal power from a motivation of fear and inadequacy, instead of self-love and self-confidence, we find ourselves becoming stressed out, overwhelmed, and even burnt out.

We need a healthy Solar Plexus Chakra so that we have the energy to use our personal power to be of service to the world we live in.

The Solar Plexus Chakra Healing Technique uses self-awareness to help you increase your mental and energetic self-love.

<u>Solar Plexus Healing Technique</u>

Step #1. Come into a comfortable sitting or lying down position. Take a few mindful breaths by bringing your attention to fully feeling your inhalations and your exhalations.

Step #2. Bring your attention to the Solar Plexus area, just below your rib cage. Imagine a cup full of liquid sitting in your Solar Plexus center.

Step #3. Set the intention that the liquid in this cup represents the amount of unconditional self-love you feel for yourself in this moment.

Step #4. Bring your awareness to how full this 'love cup' is. Maybe there is just a little liquid in the bottom of the cup, or perhaps it is half full. It may even be full or overflowing. There is no correct level of liquid we need to have in the 'love cup.' We just want to observe our level of self-love in this present moment without opinion or judgement.

Step #5. Keep a steady and mindful awareness on the 'love cup' and notice what you feel without attachment. If there is grief, disappointment, or a sense of sadness when connecting with your sense of self-love, just let those emotions be present.

Step #6. Set the intention that the liquid in the 'love cup' is rising, and that this is representing an expansion of your sense of self-love. Keep observing the 'love cup' in your Solar Plexus chakra and watch what happens.

Step #7. Spend 5 or 10 minutes observing and noticing the 'love cup.' Pay attention to how the liquid level changes as you observe it. When you feel like you have spent enough time observing your

sense of self-love bring your attention back to your breath and notice how your mind and body feels.

Women, the Media & Misogyny

Every day, as women, the media tells us we aren't enough. We are told there are ways we need to act, look, and be, if we are going to be considered attractive, sexy, and worthy. Over the course of a woman's life this message is presented to her so consistently and persistently that her Solar Plexus Chakra becomes damaged, even if she intellectually knows these messages are wrong.

Our sense of self-worth is never going to come from looking or acting a certain way. There are no changes we will ever make to the way our body looks that will make us feel inherently worthy. Our sense of self-love has to come from how we feel inside, not how we look on the outside.

When approaching Solar Plexus Chakra healing please be compassionate and gentle with yourself. The soul patterning for women, and often for men as well, that we aren't good enough the way we are runs deep, and is also still being programmed into us on a daily basis through the images and words the media pummels us with.

110

Chapter Eighteen

Heart Chakra

The fourth chakra, the Heart Chakra, is located in the energy field in the center of the chest. The Heart Chakra is our connection to the collective consciousness of love.

> The Heart Chakra is much more than our center for romantic love. It is how we channel the renewable resource of Universal Love.

It is through the information being channeled in the Heart Chakra that we communicate to the world that we want to be of service.

Our personal Heart Chakra is bigger than our bodies. It is infinite and connect us to everything. This connection to the collective, when it occurs, is a beautiful alignment in the Heart Chakra.

However, it is hard for many of us to open to this opportunity of connection because we've experienced so much trauma in our lives. These traumatic experiences have stymied our Heart Chakra's ability to be open and connected.

This is why we have to work with the Heart Chakra very gently, and also very slowly. If you are being affected by Heart Chakra

trauma, this can manifest through upper-middle back pain (between the shoulder blades), or intense left shoulder pain.

Spending time healing the Heart Chakra is definitely worth it.

When we are more open than we presently are in our Heart Chakra, we will:

- be more loving to others
- feel more being loved by others offered to us
- feel connected to humanity as a whole
- feeling optimistic that change is possible
- find enjoyment in the mundane, everyday moments of our life
- easily see the beauty in everything

Gratitude and a sense of purpose for being a soul in a human body emerges when our Heart Chakra grows and becomes aligned with the collective healing of the planet.

The Heart Chakra Healing Technique uses visualization and intention setting to clear old patterning and blockages in the Heart Chakra so that it can open wider and touch the whole world.

Heart Chakra Healing Technique

Step #1. Come into a comfortable sitting or lying down position. Take a few mindful breaths by bringing your attention to fully feeling your inhalations and your exhalations.

Step #2. Bring your attention to your heart center and let a very wide green light fill your whole chest.

Step #3. Visualize the green light moving wider than your body. Let this green light become increasingly expansive, filling the whole room if it wants to.

Step #4. Say the words *'I love myself, I accept myself, I forgive myself,'* in your mind, then send the energy of these words into the green light and towards your heart center.

Step #5. If the words *'I love myself, I accept myself, I forgive myself'* cause you stress, just release the stress by purposely slowing your breathing and lowering your shoulders. Ensure that you are in a relaxed state, and try again to send the words *'I love myself, I accept myself, I forgive myself'* into your heart center.

Step #6. Don't rush through this process. Remain sitting or lying down. Breathe for a little while. See if you can sense some tingling sensations arising in your chest area or other areas of your body.

Step #7. Notice how your body, heart and mind feel. To complete the technique bring your attention back to your breath for a few rounds of inhalations and exhalations.

Trying to Protect Your Heart

There is good reason most of us have a closed Heart Chakra that remains small instead of coming into its full expansion. We either consciously or subconsciously think that having a closed heart will protect us from being hurt.

The problem with this safety plan is that we're actually causing ourselves more hurt when we keep our heart small and closed because we cut ourselves off from giving and receiving the true amount of love available to us. This causes a sense of loneliness, abandonment and isolation to be the programming in our systems, and this hurts us just as much, or even more than, opening our heart and being disappointed.

Intentionally working with the Heart Chakra for the purpose of healing is a very deep process and can easily leave you feeling raw and exposed. You might find yourself feeling quite tender when you engage in Heart Chakra healing.

Just be gentle with yourself.

It is okay to have a soft and tender heart because it is through your own tender, soft heart that you will connect with your life purpose and find ways to be of service to this humanity you are a part of.

Chapter Nineteen

Throat Chakra

The Throat Chakra is the fifth chakra and is located in the energy field in the center of the throat. The Throat Chakra is responsible for the expression of our most authentic self.

> What or who our authentic self is really isn't that obvious. This is a normal part of the soul path process.

Feeling safe and comfortable being our authentic selves is the true challenge of the Throat Chakra. But how are we even supposed to know what our authentic self is? Let alone express it. It is normal that this really isn't that obvious.

Healing our lives, walking the soul path, and creating optimal flow in our chakras will never be a straightforward process. It will always be at least a bit challenging, full of surprises, and will generally entail mysterious events we will never fully understand.

It's important to remember that this confusion is normal. This sense that we really don't know what is happening in our lives will probably never go away. We will never be able to plan how to be our most authentic selves.

In order to heal the Throat Chakra we need to not focus on it too much. Stress and pressure will never efficiently develop confident self-expression. A better route for Throat Chakra healing is to focus on all of the other chakras, and get them aligned and healthy. When the Throat Chakra does open, our truest desires spill forth.

The Throat Chakra Healing Technique asks you to focus on the unknown. We use intention to connect with past life trauma for the purpose of healing all the old pain we no longer need so we can feel free to live our authentic truth in this present life.

Throat Chakra Healing Technique

Step #1. Come into a comfortable sitting or lying down position. Take a few mindful breaths by bringing your attention to fully feeling your inhalations and your exhalations.

Step #2. Set the intention in your mind: *"Any trauma from past lives presently affecting my throat chakra is clearing."*

Step #3. Bring your attention to your throat, and the space around your throat, and visualize dark, congested energy coming out of your body, throat chakra, and energy field, going all the way out the

(real or imaginary) window and turning back into clear, neutral energy.

Step #4. Check your throat and the energy around your throat for dark cords. If you see any dark cords then visualize them being cut by a hand or just dissolving completely. The goal is for the energy in the Throat Chakra to feel and look clear and full of light. Clear anything you see that feels dark, too attached, or unnecessary.

Step #5. Stay with the movement of the energy in your Throat Chakra and keep setting the intention: *"Any trauma from past lives presently affecting my throat chakra is clearing."* Be thorough in moving all darkness, cords, and congested energy out of your system and back to neutral energy.

Step #6. When you feel like the clearing is complete or you have done enough for now, return your attention to your breath and relax.

Step #7. Notice how you feel in your body, energy, heart, and mind.

The Narrow Channel

Our Throat Chakra represents the energy of the narrow channel between our lower survival chakras and our upper spiritual chakras. Understanding that this is a narrow channel helps us remember how patient we need to be with ourselves when engaging in Throat Chakra healing.

There is no way to efficiently shove large amounts of material through a narrow opening. It has to be done slowly and carefully. The narrow channel of the Throat Chakra asks of us to move information in and out of our systems patiently while holding a compassionate awareness. The process of aligning with our authentic self and sharing that self with the world takes time.

Past life trauma healing can be a deeper process than it seems at first. If there is crying, shaking, sweating, or other physical symptoms that occur when setting the intention to clear past life trauma, remember that this is normal. It is a positive sign that the technique is working, as the physical release tells you that old material is clearing from your Throat Chakra. If any symptoms are painful, or are concerning to you, don't hesitate to reach out to appropriate people for support.

Chapter Twenty

<u>Brow Chakra</u>

The sixth chakra, the Brow Chakra, is often called the third eye because of its location in the energy field in the middle of the forehead.

The Brow Chakra helps us to trust our own wisdom and feel confident about our own dreams.

Your Brow Chakra pertains to your perception and your way of seeing. It is through your Brow Chakra that you connect with your spiritual beliefs, your ability to be a visionary, and your alignment with your mind.

The Brow Chakra is the birthing ground of our dreams and inspirations. When we access the data in the Brow Chakra with an open willingness, our creativity shines out into the world.

What IS NOT beneficial for optimal functioning of the Brow Chakra is:

- doubt
- worry
- over-planning
- fretting

- self-criticizing
- micromanaging our lives
- imagining worst case scenarios

What IS beneficial for optimal functioning of the Brow Chakra is:

- daydreaming
- contemplation
- meditation
- visualization
- letting go of outcome
- perceiving and sensing, versus having to 'know'

The Brow Chakra Healing Technique is an opportunity for you to get your Brow Chakra into a healthy position so you can vibrationally manifest what you really want and what your soul path truly needs.

Brow Chakra Healing Technique

Step #1. Come into a comfortable sitting or lying down position. Take a few mindful breaths by bringing your attention to fully feeling your inhalations and your exhalations.

Step #2. Bring your attention to your forehead, and notice how your forehead feels. Does your forehead feel tight and like it is all wrinkled? Or does it feel loose and open? See if you can let your shoulders drop down so you can increase your sense of relaxation and loosen the tension in your forehead and in the energy field around your forehead.

Step #3. Imagine the Brow Chakra as a purple or violet light just beyond your forehead. Set the intention that the Brow Chakra is being pulled in close to your body. Imagine that all your overthinking about the future that has your Brow Chakra shooting too far forward is being pulled closer to your body. See this as a purple light hovering just next to the skin on your forehead.

Step #4. Once the purple light of the Brow Chakra feels nice and close to your physical body send the light sideways to the right and to the left so that there is a purple light stretching the whole length of your forehead and also going half a foot out on either side of your head.

Step #5. Keep your attention on the purple light, while continuing to ensure you are relaxed. If you would like you could say the statement in your mind's eye: *"I am here in the now."* Our creativity, dreams, and visions don't happen in the future—they happen now.

Step #6. Stay in this energetic alignment with your Brow Chakra for 5 to 10 minutes.

Step #7. When the energy healing feels complete return your attention to noticing your breath. Notice how your body, energy, heart and mind feel.

Worrying, Overthinking and All The Stuff That Doesn't Work

Overthinking is the most normal thing in the world. We want our life to go well, so we think about all the things that are not going well in an attempt to solve them. Many of us do this ALL THE TIME.

Just because this is normal doesn't mean it's good for us. Worrying and overthinking won't leave our lives on their own. We have to be diligent in how we use our minds if we want to make the switch from ruminating about every little detail of our lives to being more intentional about how we use our powerful minds.

One way we can do this is through purposeful engagement with the Brow Chakra. Whenever you feel yourself getting too caught up in overthinking or worrying about the future, just visualize yourself

pulling your Brow Chakra closer to your body. Feel your Brow Chakra nice and close, and feel yourself experiencing the moment as it is. This will help you reprogram the soul patterning of overthinking when it occurs.

Chapter Twenty-One

<u>Crown Chakra</u>

The seventh chakra, or Crown Chakra, is located above our heads and is our connection to the Divine, Source, God, whatever you want to call the Universal benevolent force that is bigger and greater than our individual being.

There is a benevolent support system greater than us and available to us at all times. Opening to the Crown Chakra allows us to connect to this reality.

This Universal benevolent force that all religions and many cultures speak about is an incredible source of support when we are available to it. When we are open and flowing through the Crown Chakra, we understand that we aren't alone.

In their book, *Creating on Purpose*, Anodea Judith and Lion Goodman explain:

> "When your chakras are aligned, you have the most direct access to Source, however you may define Source (within yourself, outside yourself, or both simultaneously). Just as you hold a glass

under the tap so it can be filled, we align with Source by facing into it, turning our attention toward it, and opening our 'vessel' in the most direct way possible to receive whatever we are seeking (or whatever Source has in mind)."

The Crown Chakra is a magnificent source of power that we will never fully comprehend. Crown Chakra healing requires us to accept that we will never know exactly what is going to happen in the future, even one minute from now. We need to acknowledge this truth and let go of constantly trying to control everything. People sometimes use the words truth, faith, or grace to describe this state of being or ability to let go.

Crown Chakra healing is all about being open to the moment, which takes courage, but doesn't take effort. It requires far more effort to block the moment as it is, then it does to surrender to it. It takes practice to allow life to be the *way* it is.

The Crown Chakra Healing Technique releases any blockages, cords, or darkness preventing our connection to the greater benevolent forces.

Crown Chakra Healing Technique

Step #1. Come into a comfortable sitting or lying down position. Take a few mindful breaths by bringing your attention to fully feeling your inhalations and your exhalations.

Step #2. Shift your attention to the space above your head. Imagine a funnel of light with the narrow side towards your head and the wide side facing up into infinite space.

Step #3. If there is resistance to this funnel of light being wide and bright, set the intention that any dark, congested energy is being cleared and all cords in the Crown Chakra are being cut and dissolved.

Step #4. Keep your attention on the open funnel of light and increase its strength and brightness through your loving awareness.

Step #5. If you want to strengthen this healing process you can use the words, *"I am open and available,"* and place them in your Crown Chakra.

Step #6. Stay with being aware of the light in your Crown Chakra for at least 5 or 10 minutes.

Step #7. When you feel ready to finish with this technique bring your attention back to your breath. Notice how your mind, heart, energy and body feel.

It Is Time to Ask For What You Want

Once we have acknowledged that we can set intentions in our energetic systems to create the circumstances we want in our life, we can now do this as often as we want.

The Crown Chakra is a powerful manifestation center of our systems and the collective consciousness as a whole. We can literally put a message in a bottle and send it out to the Universal seas through the Crown Chakra. If we stay open it will be received. We don't know when or how, but it will be received. And the message doesn't even need to be in a bottle.

First, you need to admit to yourself what you really want, and then you need to ask for it.

The Crown Chakra is available to you every minute of every day. Tell it what you really want by placing your words and dreams straight into the funnel of light above your head, and then sit back and watch what the tides bring to you.

Chapter Twenty-Two

Using the Chakras to

Increase theEase in Our Lives

The details of our life reflect the energetic functioning of the chakras. When the chakras are aligned, we know what we want on a soul level, and acquiring them becomes easier.

> The chakras are dynamic, ever-changing energy centers which are constantly reacting to our external world.

When we're open to working intentionally with our energy field and chakras, we have many tools at our disposal to move towards a life of good health and opportunity.

The truth is, whether we acknowledge it or not, we are actually constantly working with our chakras, just as we are with our energy field, vibration, and intention. By consciously acknowledging the ways in which the chakras influence our well-being, we can become further aligned with our soul's purpose.

Intentionally acknowledging and working with our chakra system aids us to feel more at ease with our life, which is important because life can be difficult and we need all the support we can get.

Living in the human world is inherently full of confusion and challenge. Working with the chakras doesn't erase this reality, but it does give us the capacity to make purposeful choices based on intention, love, and healing while steering away from the tendency to be guided by fear, ignorance, and frustration.

We don't need to study the chakra system for decades to tap into their power. A simple daily practice of sending energy to our chakras can bring us a renewed sense of ease, energy, and purpose to our lives.

Several years ago, I was on a trip with my mother and my young children in Alaska when energetic chakra self healing really saved me.

On this particular trip I was having a lot of difficulty sleeping and was finding myself quite tired. On the last night of the trip I was feeling pretty worried about my level of exhaustion because I knew I had to be alert and present to drive my family the safely on the long trip home the next morning.

Of course, the sense of worry I was experiencing made it more difficult for me get to sleep. I decided that, instead of fretting, I would do some chakra healing.

I fell asleep just as I completed the healing on my Crown Chakra, and even though I only got a few hours of rest, when I woke up I felt full of vitality and energy.

134

I had expected to be tired and cranky due to the lack of sleep, but as we were waiting for the ferry I felt giddy and was in a terrific mood even though it was crazy early in the morning.

What was even more remarkable was that my daughter had a full-blown tantrum, and this didn't change my mood at all! I found myself laughing and joking around the whole time, even as she was freaking out. I never even came close to losing my patience.

This event convinced me that self healing through chakra work is really one of the most accessible and effective ways to find more ease in our lives.

If you want to be able to reliably access chakra healing you will need to practice the Daily Full Chakra System Healing Technique at least a handful of times in order to feel competent with it. The ultimate goal of this healing technique is to get all the chakras spinning evenly so that any pain or trauma lodged in the seven chakras that is causing blockages can clear.

Like a little rock clogged in a gear, the pain in your system will dislodge when the chakra is spinning with force.

Daily Full Chakra System Healing Technique

Step #1. Come into a comfortable sitting or lying down position. Take a few mindful breaths by bringing your attention to fully feeling your inhalations and your exhalations.

Step #2. Bring your attention to your Root Chakra, just below your pelvis. Imagine your Root Chakra however you prefer—some see it as a hula hoop, others see a tornado/vortex, or a sphere. Sometimes people visualize the chakras as colours, or you may just want to focus on feeling the humming vibration in the chakra region. Experiment with different ways of visualizing and perceiving your chakras and find a way that is most natural for you. When you are ready, set the intention that your Root Chakra is spinning. Keep visualizing and sensing your Root Chakra, increasing its speed as you do.

Step #3. Set the intention that any pain or trauma in the Root Chakra is clearing. Keep using your mind to increase the spinning force of the Root Chakra. Imagine the darkness, congestion, pain, and trauma flying out of the Root Chakra and clearing back to neutral energy.

Step #4. Move up the chakra system and, one by one, do this same technique for the Sacral, Solar Plexus, Heart, Throat, Brow, and Crown Chakras.

Step #5. Take your time with this technique. Try to be thorough with each chakra really setting the intention for clearing, and ensuring each chakra is spinning smoothly and optimally.

Step #6. After you have completed the clearing in all of the seven major chakras, return your attention to breath and just relax.

Step #7. Notice how you feel in your body, mind, heart, and energy.

138

Chapter Twenty-Three

Let's Not Forget About the

Chakras on Your Feet

One of the reasons many of us feel alone, and like we are struggling, is that we aren't leaning into the support of the earth nearly as much as we could.

The chakras on the bottoms of our feet are an amazing resource. When open, our feet chakras allow us to be grounded, centered, connected and supported.

We can increase the support we are receiving from the earth by working intentionally with the minor chakras on the soles of our feet.

On the bottoms of each of our feet, we have two nickel-sized chakras. These Feet Chakras function as portals connecting us through our root system into the earth. When these chakras are open and activated, we have the capacity to channel life force energy from the center of the earth into our physical and energetic system.

This is a great source of renewable energy we can all tap into, but

we mostly don't. The main reason we aren't as connected to earth energy as we could be is because we are carrying too much stress on our shoulders.

You know that expression; "Carrying the world on your shoulders?" Well, it's not just an expression. It's the actual energetic alignment that gets created in our systems when we constantly worry about our lives, other people's lives, and the state of the world.

Most of us have our relationship with the earth backwards. Instead of our energetic system resting on the earth, most people have the earth resting on their shoulders. A reverse energetic pull occurs when we carry the weight of the world on our shoulders. This reverse energetic pull drags our whole body and energy system up off of the earth.

No wonder we are so tired and exhausted. We are disconnected from the energy source we need to survive and thrive.

As a result of this reverse gravitational pull, we may feel:

- spacey
- easily overwhelmed
- like our lives are unmanageable
- lonely
- pessimistic

140

- hopeless
- cynical
- despairing

Just consider plants and trees, they can't survive without the nutritional and life force energy the earth provides, and neither can we. We all need oxygen, food, and water to stay alive. These are all sourced from the earth.

We aren't here to support the earth. The earth is here to support us!

In her book *Intuitive Self Healing*, Marie Manuchehri explains:

> "The word 'grounding' in energy medicine means to receive healing, life-force energy from the earth into your body. Several small chakras are located on the bottom of both your feet, just below the surface of the skin. When a person is grounding, these small chakras release invisible energetic roots through the feet deep into the earth. Once the roots reach the core of the earth, they stop growing. The roots burrow deep within the core and act like straws receiving life sustaining energy pulling it into the first chakra."

The Earth Energy Healing Technique can be done anywhere, and at any time to ground you to the moment and receive the support of earth energy to help you through whatever you are experiencing.

Earth Energy Healing Technique

Step #1. Come into a comfortable standing position or choose a sitting position where your feet can be flat on the floor. Take a few mindful breaths by bringing your attention to fully feeling your inhalations and your exhalations.

Step #2. Bring your attention to the bottom of your right foot. Imagine a small nickel sized circle on the ball of your foot and visualize it opening like the aperture of a camera lens twisting open.

Imagine roots coming out of the open hole of your foot chakra. See the roots getting thicker and stronger as they travel down into the center of the earth. Let the roots touch the red hot core of the earth. Use the roots like straws, sucking the red, hot, life force energy up the roots, into your foot, and through your whole body.

Next imagine a nickel sized chakra on the heel of your right foot.

142

Do the same process of sending the roots down to the center of the earth and bringing the life force energy into your foot and body.

Step #3. Repeat step #2 on your left foot.

Step #4. Spend 5 to 15 minutes, or as long as you want, pulling the earth energy up from the center of the earth with your roots into your feet and up through your entire body.

Step #5. If you want you can send the earth energy into your seven major chakras.

Step #6. When the technique feels complete return your attention to your breath. Notice how your body, energy, heart and mind feel.

Staying Connected to Earth

In order to find stability and optimal health in our lives we need to be supported by the earth. Staying in constant connection with earth energy is possible if we are willing to stay grounded. This is a new soul pattern we need to create. We can do this by continually re-connecting to earth energy when we notice we've lost our

connection. Walking barefoot on the earth outside can also help keep your connection to earth energy strong.

Chapter Twenty-Four

Caring for the Body

The loving care of our body is an essential part of our soul path.

There are many resources out there about how to ensure we are getting the best sleep possible, exercising properly, and eating the healthiest foods, so I won't go into detail about those topics.

We are made up of more than our energy, chakras and vibration. We are also our bodies.

But I really want you to remember that walking the soul path requires you to take excellent care of the structure that houses your soul. This structure is your body.

One of the essential ways to care for your body is to pay careful consideration to how your body is responding to stress.

Our bodies are designed to react effectively to stress, but if we aren't actually in danger this stress response, that is meant to help us, can actually end up hurting us.

Peter A. Levine, developer of Somatic Experiencing and author of *Waking the Tiger: Healing Trauma* explains:

"In response to threat and injury, animals, including humans, execute biologically based, non-conscious action patterns that prepare them to meet the threat and defend themselves. The very structure of trauma, including activation, dissociation and freezing are based on the evolution of survival behaviors. When threatened or injured, all animals draw from a "library" of possible responses. We orient, dodge, duck, stiffen, brace, retract, fight, flee, freeze, collapse, etc. All of these coordinated responses are somatically based- they are things that the body does to protect and defend itself. It is when these orienting and defending responses are overwhelmed that we see trauma."

Trauma is another word we can use to refer to our soul patterning response to fear and danger. We can find clues to where our trauma is stored in our body through paying attention to the physiological responses we are having to the world around us.

By tuning into how our body is responding to our daily lives, we can learn a lot about what intentions we are setting, what soul patterns we are programming and which energetic self healing techniques would help us the most.

Dr. Marsha Lucas explains:

> "The state of your body is connected to your state of mind, through your brain. It's also true in the other direction: your state of mind is connected to your body state. The less aware you are of what's going on in your body, and the more it just 'does its thing' unchecked, the more likely that your basic, primitive, reflexive body states are going to be running the show…"

We don't want our basic, primitive, reflexes to be running our life. We want our wisest self who is conscious that we are on a soul path to be making intentional choices about how we react to difficult situations. This is the whole point of acknowledging that we are walking our soul path. That our choices matter!

The reaction our body is having to our environment is constantly informing our mind about what to think, and therefore sending intention to our energy which emanates out as vibrational information.

We are one interconnected system of body, intention, mind, energy, and vibration, and we need to treat ourselves accordingly. Being able to control how our body reacts to stress in a purposeful manner is an essential skill that will help you create intentional results on your soul path.

Reacting to stress in and of itself is not a problem. We will always experience stress as souls in a human body, and we need our body to have this innate ability to cope with risk and danger.

But we also want to use this physiological reaction to stress appropriately, and only when it's actually needed.

If your body is telling you that you are in danger, let's say a car is driving quickly towards you, and you need to move fast so you don't get hit, this stress response is justified, since it's literally saving your life. When used appropriately, the physiological survival response is something to celebrate.

Usually when we're stressed out though, our life isn't actually in danger. Maybe we've forgotten to charge our cell phone or are late for an appointment, or something mundane like that. These situations are not life-threatening.

However, we often freak out when small things aren't going right. It is our own freaking out that is telling our body and mind that we are in danger, which then greatly taxes our physical, emotional, mental, and energetic systems.

This is one of the reasons we need to use Mindfulness in our lives. We need to be aware of where our attention is so that we can notice when we're having a physiological fear response to a situation that is not necessarily life-threatening.

A physiological fear response looks like:

- sweating
- trembling
- hot flushes or chills
- shortness of breath or difficulty breathing
- a choking sensation
- rapid heartbeat (tachycardia)
- pain or tightness in the chest
- a sensation of butterflies in the stomach
- nausea
- headaches and dizziness
- feeling faint
- numbness or pins and needles
- dry mouth
- a need to go to the toilet
- ringing in your ears
- confusion or disorientation

When we are mindful that our body is inappropriately reacting by having a physiological fear response to a situation that is not life threatening, we have a great opportunity for healing. When we are aware this is happening we have the opportunity to re-program this inappropriate physiological response by telling ourselves that we are safe.

Purposefully telling ourselves we are safe is a necessary step of our soul healing process. When we do this we change our deeply ingrained soul patterning in that moment.

The more we let our body and mind believe our life is in danger when it's actually not, the more we strengthen the soul patterning of over-reacting to mundane situations.

Having physiological survival responses really wears us down. If we don't need to have such a strong reaction in order to survive, it is best not to, because over using our physiological fear responses is the fastest way to become sick, burnt out, and feel like you can't cope with your life.

The challenge is that your body is mostly unable to tell the difference between being safe and being in danger, because its sense of safety is a mental interpretation. You need to use the mind itself as a tool to tell the body when you are safe. Mostly you are safe. Let's give your body this information!

"I am safe" is a powerful affirmation you can use any time. Saying *"I am safe"* when you are triggered by stress and fear, or are simply feeling anxious, scared, or worried, supports the Root Chakra, which is the base support for all of your life experiences.

When our systems believe they are in physical danger, we often become jumpy and reactive. This agitation in the system makes it very difficult to stay calm and centered, and is a common cause of

150

easily snapping at people, making irrational decisions, and eventually becoming exhausted.

Our bodies weren't created to function constantly on high alert. When these physiological reactions to fear are 'on' all the time, we'll get worn out.

To counteract our bodies' sense of needing to be on high-alert to danger too often, we need to reassure it that we are safe. The easiest way to communicate to our bodies that we are safe is with our breath.

Using the Breath to Calm Our Bodies Down

One of the first things that can happen when we're stressed is that our breathing becomes short and shallow. Shallow breathing is a message to the body that we are in danger. To change how we are communicating to the body in times of stress, we need to change our breathing. When we choose to purposely slow down and deepen our breathing, our body gets the message that it's safe.

When you notice you are stressed, sit somewhere quietly for a moment, close your eyes, and just breathe slow and deep. If your brain keeps trying to make a decision about how to react to the

stress you're experiencing, slow down your breathing even more, and make sure your breathing pattern is even before giving the decision further thought.

This is one way to ensure your decision-making is coming from a sense of safety, rather than from a reactive place of fear and danger. If you're walking instead of sitting, you can slow your pace. Changing your physical movement to one of being slow and steady also changes the signals you are sending to your body about your state of safety in the world.

We all need to learn to calm down, and working with our breath is one way we can do this.

We can also recognize that we've been conditioned by society to be in a constant state of accelerated stress. We are continually being told we need to buy more, make more money, do more activities etc.

This outside pressure to always be achieving can really put strain on our systems. This strain can be released. When you release the accumulated stress that has built up over this life and all of your past lives, you will notice yourself feeling calmer, more neutral, and less reactive in many situations.

The Releasing Stress from the Shoulders Energetic Healing Technique can be used at the end of a stressful day to release the

accumulated stress you are holding on to, or can be used in the actual moment you are having a stressful reaction to alter your reactive soul patterning before it sets in deeper.

Releasing Stress from the Shoulders

Healing Technique

Step #1. Come into a comfortable sitting, standing, or lying down position. Take a few mindful breaths by bringing your attention to fully feeling your inhalations and your exhalations.

Step #2. Visualize a tall column of heavy darkness above both of your shoulders. This dark column represents the stress you are carrying. See how high the column goes. (It might go all the way to the ceiling or beyond!)

Step #3. Visualize the heavy, dark column above your right shoulder being pushed down. See the column getting smaller. Keep going until the column has been pushed all the way down through your body and out your feet into the earth.

Step #4. Repeat Step #3 on your left shoulder.

Step #5. Bring your attention back to your shoulders and see if there is still any dark heaviness remaining above your shoulders. If any trace of a dark column still remains on either shoulder repeat step #3 on one or both shoulders.

Step #6. Notice how your shoulders feel.

Step #7. Return your attention to your breath and relax.

Chapter Twenty-Five

Do We Need to Protect Ourselves from Negative Energy?

One of the main questions people ask me as an energy healer is how they can protect themselves from other people's negative energy.

This is a very common concern and fear, and the simplest answer I can give is; you don't have to.

> No other person can make your energy negative.

No one else can 'make' you feel negative.

It is only your reactions to situations that cause negativity. This is a truth of the soul path. We, ourselves are the ones causing our energy to be positive or negative even though this is not how it feels.

When people are mean to us, criticize us, or are cruel towards us, it really feels like we are being treated negatively and that this is the other person's fault.

You are not just imagining that this is how it feels when you are being treated badly. It *does* feel like other people are giving us their negative energy. And maybe they are offering negativity towards us, but the real question we need to ask ourselves is; are we taking it?

155

Our energy and our vibration is being created through what we choose to focus on. When we give all of our attention to the negativity around us this is the intention we implant into our energy.

All our soul healing comes from our own willingness to take responsibility for our pain and suffering. This is what we are learning to do by intentionally walking our soul path, and this is what we need to remember when it feels like we are being affected by other people's negative energy.

This does not mean that other people haven't been disrespectful, cruel, abusive, or violent towards us. There is never an excuse for abuse, and we never want to blame the victim when violence has occurred. This is not what I am trying to state by saying we need to take responsibility for our own suffering, but this is often how this teaching gets interpreted.

Instead of blaming anyone for any negative energy that seems to be ensuing, we want to acknowledge the reality that we can't control other people's thoughts, actions, behaviours, or perspectives. We can *only* control our own thoughts, actions, behaviours or perspectives, and therefore the *only* way to change our lives is to make changes to how we are focusing our attention.

If you feel like you are 'picking up' other people's negative energy, what you are probably doing is being overly focused on the negativity of others.

156

It is our reactions that cause our pain. Our reactions are mostly neurotic and unconscious, this is true, but they're still having a powerful effect on our life.

We will never find a way to react that will always prevent us from experiencing pain, but we can become observant and aware of the way we do react to gain information as to where more soul healing needs to be done.

Taking responsibility for our own soul path means acknowledging that it is our own reactions causing our suffering, and this can often feel like too much. We can feel helpless and hopeless and like we will never find a way not to be 'picking up' the negative energy of the world.

But this isn't true. Choosing to place our attention away from negativity is an easy skill to learn. If you are as brave and courageous, and as seriously committed to healing your soul patterning as I know you are, you will find ways to turn your attention away from the negativity that you don't want to be your energetic programming.

The way to not 'pick up' negative energy or to protect yourself from negative energy is to not give it your attention. That doesn't mean being a punching bag for other people, or just ignoring abuse, it just means that your attention is going towards giving yourself love, and working towards appropriate healthy reactions to negative situations.

Not 'picking up' negative energy also requires you to focus on your positive vision for your future instead of continuing to worry about the failures of the past.

We will never be able to entirely avoid being around grumpy, cranky, disappointed, or frustrated people, or being one of these people, ourselves. These are normal feelings, and we are all going to have them sometimes.

A couple of years ago I was on pleasant scenic drive while visiting the island of Maui. Two other people were in the car with me, and I was in a very good mood. I was enjoying the leisurely feel of the day. I was loving just kicking back and relaxing while feeling the ocean breeze through my open window. But the person in the back seat of the car wasn't having the good time I was having. They were in a bad mood.

As I focused my attention on the bad mood of the person in the back seat I very quickly felt myself also slipping into a bad mood. I started to wish I was somewhere else, even though moments before I was had been having a very pleasant experience.

I decided I needed some Mindfulness to become more aware of what my attention was doing. I asked myself the two essential questions, *where is my attention now?* and *where do I want my attention now?*

It turned out my attention was on worrying about the pouting person in the backseat and being irritated that they were 'ruining' my enjoyable day. Where I wanted my attention was on noticing the beautiful day that was present in that moment.

I immediately realized that the pouting person in the back seat wasn't ruining my day at all! I was ruining my own day through how I was directing my attention. I was the one focusing on the negativity of the situation, and therefore I was causing myself to feel negative. I had all the power in this situation, not the person in the back seat.

I made the choice to internally send love and compassion to the person in the back seat and decided it was none of my business how they were feeling. Then I chose to return my attention to being in a good mood, which meant enjoying the beautiful view out the window and going back to feeling relaxed.

Everyone has the right to be in a bad mood if that is the way they feel, and by not taking responsibility for other people's bad moods we give them the space to feel as they need to without more negativity being directed towards them in the form of resentment or disappointment.

Our purpose in life isn't to 'fix' anyone else, make anyone else feel better, or prevent others from having discomfort, even the people we love most. Most of us are utterly confused and mystified about

our own path, so how can we possibly know what other people need?

Walking the soul path is a solo journey, but we do share it with billions of other humans. One of the things about sharing the planet with everyone else is that sometimes we come into contact with other people's energy.

This is why we need to be intentional about how we hold our energy when we are around other people. Most people hold their energy fields too far away from their bodies, which causes their energy field to come into contact with more energetic information than is necessary. When our energy field is too far from our bodies we can easily become overwhelmed and exhausted throughout our day.

Our energy field is like a bubble or cocoon around our body. Our energy field is also always changing position. It can sit close to our body or far away. Your energy field is picking up information in your vicinity, so working with the energy field is one of the ways we can choose not to get entangled with negativity that is happening around us.

Just imagine, if your energy field is positioned far away from your body and you work in a busy office building or are walking down a street where you are close to other people, your energy field is picking up too much information. This is one reason so many

people feel overwhelmed or ungrounded because their energy field is too far away from their bodies. Maybe this is happening to you?

Pulling in the energy field is one of the best skills we can learn in order to feel safe and secure in our energy and around other people's energies.

The Pulling in Your Energy Field Technique takes practice but once you get good at it you will be able to rely on it to help you in many situations.

Pulling in Your Energy Field

Healing Technique

Step #1. Come into a comfortable standing position (if standing isn't an option sitting in a chair works, too). Take a few mindful breaths by bringing your attention to fully feeling your inhalations and your exhalations.

Step #2. Visualize your energy field as light all around your body.

Step #3. Send the light as far away from your body as possible, filling the whole room you are in with your light.

161

Step #4. Pull your energy field in close to your body by visualizing the light of your energy field coming very close to your body.

Step #5. Make sure to pull the energy field down at your head, in from your sides, and in on your back, too.

Step #6. Stand still. Breathe.

Step #7. Notice how your body, mind and energy feels.

Why You Should Pull In Your Energy Field

I had a student once who lived in a very isolated spot in the bush and was rarely around other people. One day she went to the big hardware store in the city near where she lived and experienced symptoms that were common to her when she was around large groups of people; she became dizzy, confused and even a little faint.

Usually when these symptoms would occur she would leave the store without completing her shopping. But this time she had just completed a course I used to offer called Taking Care of Your

Energy Field and Chakras Course, and she decided that instead of leaving the store immediately upon feeling these symptoms, she would just pull in her energy field. She pulled in her energy field and instantly the dizziness subsided and she found herself grounded and focused. She was able to finish her shopping without feeling overwhelmed or ill in any way.

I also used to find myself in situations where I was having physical symptoms of feeling anxious such as: butterflies in my stomach, heart beating fast, and being out of breath when I was around certain people. I started to wonder if maybe other people around me were feeling anxious and I was picking up their feelings through our energy fields coming into contact. I decided to test this theory out.

One day I was walking with a friend and I started to feel this sense of anxiety for no reason. I wondered if my friend might be anxious in that moment. I pulled in my energy field and my own anxiety symptoms immediately dissipated.

These are two perfect examples of how we can use self-awareness, mindfulness and energetic self healing techniques to benefit our lives even in the midst of uncomfortable situations.

Chapter Twenty-Six

Letting Go of Perfect

There was a time in my life when it pained me to realize I wasn't perfect. As a naive 20-year-old, somehow I thought that this was what I was supposed to be — perfect. And by perfect, I mean someone who did everything right, never made a mistake, and was loved by everyone.

> Walking our soul path doesn't mean trying to be perfect.

It wasn't that I was supposed to *become* perfect sometime in the future. It was that I thought I was somehow supposed to be innately perfect, as in born flawless.

But I wasn't this way, and this bugged me.

I found it painful to live in the daily reality of my own imperfection. I thought this was a problem. Actually, I thought *I* was a problem. I was sure that my entire life was going to be ruined because of my own inability to do almost anything correctly. I was constantly aware of my own imperfections and this caused me to feel anxious and uncomfortable in my own skin.

165

Thinking that we need to be perfect in order to be loveable is an old soul patterning that many of us need to work on reversing.

When we think that the only way we will be loveable and feel safe in the world is by getting everything 'right' all the time, we find ourselves living in a constant state of fear of making mistakes.

Maybe if I make a mistake no one will want to be around me? This is a fear many of us have. This can be very painful because then, when we do make mistakes, our inner voice is quick to remind us about how imperfect and unlovable we are. Then we experience more anxiety and discomfort and our life is not very fun and enjoyable. This is no way to walk our soul path, especially because there is no way *not* to make mistakes when we're a soul in a human body.

Walking our soul path is not about pushing ourselves to be perfect on our journey. Perfect is not possible, so setting this unrealistic goal is only going to cause us more pain then necessary on our path.

Instead of looking for perfection on our soul path, we can work towards embracing unconditional self-love; which means loving ourselves without any conditions.

Striving for perfect will never make us feel good about ourselves. When we close the door on perfection and welcome in unconditional love, we allow ourselves to fall in love with the

moment and ourselves as we are, full of all the flaws that make this soul path so interesting.

Loving ourselves is actually quite easy when things are going well. But what about when we are sick, scared, confused, or feeling unattractive? This is when we can quickly turn our backs on ourselves.

I believe we are given difficult and varied circumstances to experience on our soul's path so we can develop an ability to internally align with unconditional self-love, not only in times where we're having success, but also in those tough times we all experience.

This is not easy; but it is possible.

Here are some questions we can ask ourselves to help us strengthen our internal alignment of unconditional self-love:

Would I love myself if I weighed 50 pounds more than I do now? How about 100 pounds more?

Would I love myself if I declared bankruptcy and lost my house?

Would I love myself if I was fired from my job or my spouse left me?

Would I love myself if I didn't have use of my legs, or needed help to use the bathroom?

And of course, these aren't hypothetical questions. These are realities for many people (maybe even you). There is also a good

chance you might have one of these experiences in your future.

We are afraid of pain, which makes sense, because it hurts. We like to think that if we are perfect, or get everything right, we won't have to experience suffering.

But as we have already determined, no one is able to prevent suffering through their actions. So, instead of making it our goal to try to be perfect and prevent suffering, we can make an active effort to benefit from every opportunity we are presented with on our soul path through the attitude we choose to embrace. We can ask ourselves:

Can I love myself no matter what happens?

For this level of unconditional love to encapsulate our life, we need to let go of all of our clinging to a dream of 'perfect'. We need to let 'perfect' completely dissolve out of our systems.

Of course, 'perfect' is not the only thing we need to let go of on our healing soul path journey. There are many old belief systems we are all hanging on to that are not serving us.

The Letting Go Healing Technique can be used for any and all old belief systems we are holding on to that are preventing us from completely embracing unconditional self-love on our soul path.

Letting Go Healing Technique

Step #1. Come into a comfortable sitting, standing or lying down position. Take a few mindful breaths by bringing your attention to fully feeling your inhalations and your exhalations.

Step #2. Think of one thing that has been stressing you out lately that you're ready to let go of. Maybe it is a person you are unnecessarily worrying about, financial issues you don't want to be concerned with anymore, or a memory from the past you feel done with.

Step #3. Visualize a strong flowing river moving quickly. Then choose an image or a word to represent the issue you want to let go of.

Step #4. In your imagination drop the word or image into the flowing river and let it float away. Do not follow it with your mind. Stay where you are and just breath.

Step #5. Notice what you feel in your body and mind.

Step #6. Repeat steps #1 to #5 with another issue if you want. Let go of as many issues as you wish.

You are You

We have all incarnated into human form to learn unconditional self-love and to repair our relationships with our own souls. The only way to learn this is through practice.

We are ourselves, right now. It doesn't matter what we weigh, how much money we have, how we look, how healthy we are, or how popular we are. We are our own being in this moment, and it is only in the here and now that we can accept and love ourselves. This is not something that can be done in the future.

Challenging circumstances don't happen because we are 'bad' in any way. They just happen because we are human, and we are human for the purpose of strengthening our internal alignment of unconditional self-love.

Chapter Twenty-Seven

The Resistance is Real

Even when we understand that walking the soul path means actively healing soul patterns so we can fully embody unconditional love, it can still be difficult to find the motivation to make the changes we need to make.

This is a normal part of the soul path. It is hard to make the actual changes we know we need to make.

> If we wait until the resistance is gone to do our soul healing work we will never do it.

It is hard, but it's not impossible. This is important to remember. We don't want to get caught up in the fact that making transformational change in our life is hard. But we also want to be cognizant of the difficult nature of soul pattern re-programming so we can stay compassionate and kind with ourselves through the entire process.

But why is it so difficult to change ourselves anyway? Well, there are many answers to that question. We will cover a few of them here.

It is difficult to create change in our life, partly because we feel safe in our neurosis and dysfunction because it's what we know.

171

The familiar feels secure, even if it isn't actually safe or healthy for us. The unknown is intrinsically scary, because it is unknown.

Resistance is what we feel when we know there are soul patterns we want to change but we don't seem to be able to make the shifts necessary to fully alter the way we are acting or thinking. This can be extremely frustrating because even though we know that our neurotic ways aren't serving us anymore, we don't seem to be able to let them go.

But Jack Canfield, the spiritual motivational speaker reminds us that:

> "Everything we want is on the other side of fear."

Resistance arises when we're working hard to change our life because pain and trauma are actually their own entities. I know this sounds weird, but stay with me.

Everything wants to survive. All animals, plants, and organisms have a survival mechanism wired into them. This is the same with trauma programming in our energetic systems. These energies of pain and trauma in our system want to survive. That is why they don't leave easily.

Eckhart Tolle explains it like this:

> "The pain-body wants to survive, just like every other entity in existence, and it can only survive if it gets you to unconsciously identify with it."

It is us believing that the pain is true that keeps it surviving. So, of course, our pain reminds us of its validity at every turn.

The way I was so sure, in my 20's, that being imperfect made me unloveable kept that pain alive in my system. The more we believe our pain and trauma is the truth, the more power it has over us, and the more it continues to want to survive.

We can't just hope or wish our pain away. Since the pain wants to survive, it has become entrenched into our systems. The pain and trauma does not want us to believe we can live without it, because it thinks that us not believing in it will be its death.

But nothing dies, everything just transforms. Our pain won't die when we let it go. Instead it will transform beautifully into new, clean energy that can be reused for something new in the future.

The pain and trauma doesn't know this, though. It doesn't know it will transform into something new and beautiful, it thinks it is going to die, so it resists being cleared.

However, it is our own opinion, not the opinion of the pain and trauma resistance that we need to listen to and be guided by on our soul path.

When we stop resonating with our pain it can easily be cleared from our system. This is not something we do with passive, wishful thinking. This is something we do with active self-awareness and energetic self healing techniques.

173

When we feel we just can't get on with the healing work, even though we know we need to do it, then we can be sure we are having an experience of resistance.

Resistance almost always occurs when we are working hard to enact change, because resistance is the pain body trying to survive. Experiencing resistance is not a sign that you are failing on your soul path. It's actually the opposite. When resistance arises, it is a sign that you're successfully making in-roads at altering your soul patterning.

Everyone experiences resistance when they try to reverse soul patterning. Maybe you've been working hard to make lifestyle changes that involve increased self-care and are finding it very difficult to sustain these changes. This sense of difficulty we experience in making the changes often makes us feel like we are failing. But we are not. We are just facing a normal part of the soul path process.

The sensation of resistance is not in your imagination. It is not just you making your life difficult or not being smart or disciplined enough. The resistance is real, and it is challenging, and it is definitely the most difficult part of walking the soul path and engaging in energetic self healing.

How Resistance Presents Itself

When we understand, intellectually, that clearing energy isn't actually the end of anything, we don't have to get caught up in the resistance. We can see the resistance but not believe it. We don't want to give resistance a voice in our healing process.

When we understand how to work with resistance, we can clear stagnant energy from our bodies, minds, and energy fields even when we know that resistance is present.

Pain is always going to be stubborn about leaving your system because it essentially fears its own death. Put another way, we are scared to really let it go because it *does* feel like a sort of death, but on the soul path there is no end and no beginning, just a continual process of energy shifting and changing.

We can get on with healing even if we are feeling the following symptoms of resistance:

- believing the healing process is too difficult

- believing nothing we try will ever change anything in our lives

- feeling like we don't have the physical energy to change our lives

- feeling foggy in the brain

- feeling hopeless, depressed, and, at its worst, suicidal

- feeling stuck

- feeling like it's impossible to make a decision

What should we do when these frustrating and uncomfortable experiences of resistance are getting in the way of us intentionally walking our soul path?

What we do is we get intimate with our resistance instead of pushing it away. When we try to get away from the resistance it only embeds deeper into our subconscious.

The resistance is real. It is a thing we all experience. But the resistance isn't *true*. You can change, and you will change. The issues bothering you can be healed.

We need to hold these truths higher than the resistance and use them to counter the challenging thoughts and experiences resistance brings into our lives.

When we understand that resistance is not the truth, we don't have to be scared of it anymore, and we don't have to let it trick us into inaction.

You will know you are an expert at working skillfully with your resistance when you come to a place where, even though resistance is uncomfortable, you accept it and continue actively walking your

soul path. When this happens you will feel empowered to tackle any and all of your soul patterning.

Once you learn to dance with resistance gracefully you can let the resistance go quickly, rather than allowing it to stop your dance.

To override the resistance you have to acknowledge that you are scared, maybe even terrified, and move towards healing anyway.

If we don't understand how to work with fear and resistance in this way, we won't heal.

If you know you are facing a lot of resistance on your soul path, use The General All Purpose Clearing Technique on Page 74 to set the intention for the resistance itself to clear out of your system. Leaning heavy on your intentions of clearing will keep the resistance moving.

Chapter Twenty-Eight
<u>Different is the Only Normal</u>

Our system employs resistance for more reasons than we would ever be able to list. The ways we as humans can be hurt, injured, destroyed, and killed is beyond what we will ever be aware of, or would ever want to be aware of. Being human is a very vulnerable form of being.

But one of the ways we as humans fear being injured or destroyed is through being cast out of the tribe due to being different. This is why many people, maybe even you, feel uncomfortable when we think we might be perceived as strange or weird.

> If you want to fully stand in the power of your soul's journey, you need to take the risk of being weird.

Making choices that make us feel different or weird can trigger anxious feelings because so many of us have a belief stored in our energetic system that being different is a dangerous way to be.

This belief is justified. Right now, all over the world people are being hurt and killed because they're perceived as different. You may have been endangered at one point in your own life because people perceived you as different, or this might even be a present fear or reality for you.

179

Teasing and bullying are examples of this, but so are racism, homophobia, anti-Semitism, Islamophobia, and misogyny, just to name a few.

Even if you have not experienced suffering in this life due to being different, you probably have experienced this type of brutality in a past life through torture, persecution, or murder.

This type of cruelty, between humans who don't agree on what 'normal' is, happens every minute of every day, all over the world. It's no wonder we fear it.

But we *are* different.

All of us are.

This is why it's really hard to heal our Throat Chakras and feel safe to be our completely authentic selves. We fear being hurt by our own species if they see us being our true selves.

Unfortunately, we have no choice on the soul path but to be our weird and different selves. This is the only person we are, so this is the only person we can be.

Yes, showing the world our weird, funky selves is scary, but we have to do it anyway. Walking the soul path asks us to make risky choices about who we are going to be, even if we're worried about what others will think of us.

No one chose to be a soul in a human body to play it safe. We incarnated as humans to change our soul patterning, which means

taking risks and stepping out of our ingrained comfort zones.

When we let the fear of being different prevent us from making choices that are going to progress us on our soul healing journey, we stagnate on our path. We need to act in ways that are really true to us, even if we are scared that no one will love us or accept us,

The fear we are experiencing is a form of resistance trying to protect us, but also trying to protect itself. This fear is blocking us from the evolution and transformation we are meant to accomplish in this incarnation.

Howard Thurman, philosopher and theologian, explains:

> "Don't ask what the world needs. Ask what makes you come alive, and go do it. Because what the world needs is people who have come alive."

No one is given their soul purpose directly and clearly. There are no instructions or to-do lists we can follow to be sure we are making good progress on our soul path. We have to discover our soul purpose ourselves, and this can only be done by not giving in to fears of being seen as weird or different.

Everything happening externally is a manifestation of what is happening internally. So, when we give the fear and resistance the option to occupy a lot of our internal space, then our external

space will become full of reflections of this fear, which can look like people in our life doubting or not supporting us.

We need to gather all of our courage in the direction of being our true, weird selves. This is what our soul path is asking us to do.

Want to be like everyone else? Then be weird.

Conquering My Own Fears of Being Weird

For myself, talking and writing freely about meditation, energy fields, and vibration has been a kind of coming out of the closet. I mean, let's admit it, to many folks, this sounds like pretty weird stuff!

I have had to work very skillfully and intentionally with my own fear and resistance in order to embrace my soul purpose as an energy healer. No external source has ever promised me that becoming an energy healer would be a definite path to success. Actually, pursuing this path as an energy healer and teacher has never felt particularly safe.

The way I have overcome the resistance and fear when it arises is in my own experience is by going for a walk alone in the woods and saying out loud, "I see you, resistance, and I'm not listening to you. I am doing what I need to do, even though there is fear and

182

anxiety present." (Can you see why I was worried about looking weird?)

Chapter Twenty-Nine

Forgiveness Allows Us
To Stay InThe Flow Of Life

We've all made choices that we are not proud of. We've all been hurt by others and, at times, been the one hurting others.

This is just the way it is; we need to get on with walking our soul path anyway, no matter what occurred in the past.

Self-forgiveness is the most efficient path to soul healing.

As we've discussed throughout this book, beating ourselves up about the soul patterns or trauma we are carrying only prevents us from getting on with the healing our soul path is asking us to do.

It's not the pain itself that's preventing us from healing. It's our lack of ability to unconditionally *accept* our pain that stops us from moving forward.

I know you might be scared that it will hurt too much to really accept your pain, but here's the thing: you're already hurting by resisting the pain. So maybe it's time to accept the pain, clear it once and for all, and become free.

There is a quote that I don't have a source for, but that for me encompasses the whole purpose of the soul path.

> "Forgive yourself. Not just once—but again, and again, and again, as many times as it takes to find peace."

These are the words of guidance we all need to hear when pondering how we should handle the pain and trauma we're constantly facing on this human journey.

People are often confused about how to do forgiveness, though. People often feel so mad at the perpetrators who've hurt them, and at themselves for the mistakes they've made that they feel it's impossible to fully embrace forgiveness. When we start to understand that there's only one person we need to forgive, and that is ourselves, forgiveness becomes the only path forward.

Eckhart Tolle explains:

> "The ego says: Maybe at some point in the future, I can be at peace – if this, that, or the other happens, or I obtain this or become that. Or it says: I can never be at peace because of something that happened in the past. Listen to people's stories and they could all be entitled "Why I Cannot Be at Peace Now." How to be at peace now? By making peace with the present moment. The present moment is the field on which the

game of life happens. It cannot happen anywhere else."

Self-Forgiveness isn't something we can conceptualize; it's something we need to actually *do*. We need to take the time to say sorry to ourselves for all the times we've told ourselves that we are ugly, dumb, or inadequate. It hurt when we said these cruel things to ourselves, and for that reason we need to apologize to ourselves and make repair with our own being.

When we forgive ourselves for everything that has occurred up to, and including, this present moment we give ourselves the opportunity to let go of the past and start living fully in the present moment.

Two common ways of dealing with personal pain that keeps the pain alive instead of healing and clearing the pain permanently are:

> *Repressing pain by putting on a big smile and pretending everything is great when it isn't.*

and

> *Completely focusing on the pain and turning it into our identity and total existence.*

Both of these ways of dealing with pain cause the pain to remain longer in our systems than necessary.

It is only when we offer our pain full unconditional acceptance and forgiveness that it can move out of our systems.

Every moment is different.

We are born, and we die, and in between we change again and again and again.

If we hold too tight to any one moment it solidifies in our energetic system and clogs up the natural flow of life. New energy is always trying to move into our systems, but if there is no room for it to do so, because the energy of the past hasn't been cleared out yet, then we become stuck between the new and the old.

When the old energy can't flow out and the new energy can't flow in, we can become frozen. Our life seems in a rut. When this happens we need to ask ourselves the question:

Am I a stagnant pond, or am I flowing river? And which one do I want to be?

If we believe we are a river, then we need to let the old energy that is no longer serving us flow downstream and away from our present life.

If we've found that we're stagnating because we haven't acknowledged our pain, or because we've allowed our pain to become our whole being, causing a log jam in the current of our energy, then what we need to do is admit to ourselves that we're suffering and let it be real, but not let it be who we are.

Then we need to let it all go by forgiving ourselves for holding on to the pain too tightly and for too long.

This process of acknowledging our pain and letting it go can't be approached with force. If we are too aggressive with trying to let go of our past we are only going to hurt ourselves more.

It is only with a gentle loving presence that we will be able to see clearly what pain needs to be unconditionally accepted and then cleared back into neutral energy.

Everything moves and everything changes. This is the challenge and opportunity life has to offer. The more we choose to see this constant change as opportunity, the more we can work with the flow and let the natural current of the river of life wash away the places we feel stuck.

When we're feeling stuck, we also need support to return to the flow of life. We need to reach out to friends, healers, and other support systems and ask them to remind us that life is a river.

We need to let the people who love us know that right now we feel stuck and ask them to remind us about how great we are and accept their encouragement to get back into the flow of life.

The soul path is not one we do alone. Always combine energetic self healing techniques with reaching out to the appropriate resources for help.

The Staying in the Flow Energetic Healing Technique will help you generate a continual flow of life force energy through your body, energy field and chakras.

Staying in the Flow Energetic Healing Technique

Step #1. Come into a comfortable sitting, standing, or lying down position and bring your attention to your breath, fully feeling your inhalations and your exhalations.

Step #2. Bring your attention to your feet and set the intention that the energy is flowing from the center of the earth through your feet and up through your entire body. Stay with this for a few breaths.

Step #3. Bring your attention to your head and set the intention that energy is coming down from the infinite sky and traveling down through your entire body. Stay with this for a few breaths.

Step #4. When you feel ready alternate between step #2 and step #3. Experience the energy coming up from the feet, and then experience the energy flowing down from the head. Go back and forth between these two energy flows. If it feels like there are blocks preventing the energy from moving, just let the energy itself move the blocks. Keep your attention on the flowing energy, not the blocks, and feel the energy flowing on its own from the bottom to the top, and from the top to the bottom of your system.

190

Step #5. Do this exercise for anywhere from 3 to 15 minutes, or longer.

Step #6. When you feel that you have completed this exercise, relax and return your attention to your breath.

Step #7. Notice how your body, mind, heart, and energy feels.

Imagining a Hot Coal

Imagine that you're holding a hot coal in your hand and it's burning you intensely. The only way for the hot coal to stop hurting you is for you to open your hand and let it go.

Holding on to anger and regret is like holding that hot coal. As long as we hold on to the anger it continues to burn us. When we say the words to ourselves, *"I love you and I forgive you,"* we drop the hot coal out of our hands and the pain we were causing ourselves stops.

Chapter Thirty

<u>Going Forward from Here</u>

I am eternally grateful for the past two decades of spiritual and soul development I have embarked on. But if I were to go back and do it again, there are few things I would do differently based on what I know now.

> When you are struggling, you can go straight to an energetic self healing technique instead of rolling the problem around in your mind trying to find a mental solution.

I wish over the last two decades I had been kinder to myself, but the experience of self-hate itself brought me great growth and learning. Through my own experience of unnecessary self-disdain and self-betrayal, I learned that self-kindness needs to be the primary force behind all healing. This is what motivates me now.

The other big waste of my time was engaging in constant doubt about if things would work out okay for me. All that spinning in doubt was just strengthening a soul pattern that I no longer need. Now I try to catch self-doubt as soon as it occurs and remind myself that it's not real.

Lastly, when I look back at my own journey I see that procrastinating doing the energetic self healing techniques that I know work to make me feel better only drags out the experience of resistance longer than is necessary.

Now when I feel myself resistant to change, I go directly to engaging in an energetic self healing technique to keep my energy as clear, and open as possible.

Energetic Self Healing in a Big Box Store

Last week I was in a big box store (that I shall not name) against my will (okay, I wasn't kidnapped -but I didn't want to be there). I was feeling really yucky being in the store so I lapped the store once, to help myself become more centered (and because I lost the person I was with). While I was walking around the store I did the Daily Full Chakra Healing Technique (page #136) .

As my chakras gained vibration and became larger and more fluid, my mood improved, and I felt more able to cope with the moment at hand.

By the time I had gone around the entire store and intentionally sent energy to all of my chakras, I was feeling solid in my high

vibration state and ready to continue on with my day in a positive state. I still didn't like being in that particular store, but my mood and energy felt positive and vibrant.

Making soul path decisions to walk away from old soul patterning that no longer serves us, and travel into the unknown is always going to include uncomfortable sensations.

The resistance is real, seeing it and not being overtaken by it will be necessary as you change your energetic system with the techniques offered in this book.

But you can do it. I have no doubt you can.

Going forward, I encourage you to open up to the entire range of your human/soul experience. That means having *all* of the emotions, *all* of the doubt and confusion, facing massive resistance, and being prepared to face all types of experiences. Everything has something to teach us.

The purpose of committing to walking the soul path is not to get this human life 'right' or to 'win' in any way. Our purpose is to make a big, royal mess through complicated choices, relationships and adventures. Get out there and experience as much as you can!

As Miss Frizzle tells us on the children's show *The Magic School Bus*:

"Take chances, make mistakes, get messy."

I hope you will find ways to use this book as a resource. The chapters are meant to be read more than once. Let the guidance in this book be a support you can return to when you feel confused or are faced with difficult challenges in your life.

In the following appendix sections you will find guides to help you choose the best energetic self healing techniques from this book for whatever you are going through.

You are the expert on your life. Anything anybody says, including me, are only suggestions. Take everything simply as guidance to help you find your way on your totally unique and incredible soul path.

As the Buddha said:

> "No one saves us but ourselves. No one can and no one may. We ourselves must walk the path."

Appendix One

Guide to Energetic Self Healing Techniques

The energetic self healing techniques I offer in this book are not just words, but a way to engage in sending purposeful intentions to your energy. Expect to feel results!

These results might feel like a new and exciting clarity or energy, but could also occur as increased exhaustion, confusion, or feeling like old pain from your past is resurfacing. And of course, there is always resistance. This is all good, even if it doesn't initially feel good. If your energetic system has been stagnant for a long time, then your system becoming stirred up is an important part of the process.

Please take good care of yourself. Make sure you are drinking enough water, eating healthy foods that support the body while it's energetically healing, and ensure you get some light exercise to keep your body in good shape. Also, it is important not to become isolated. Reach out to friends, family, and other appropriate supports to help you along the way. Energetic self healing is part of a holistic healing process, so keep taking care of your whole self!

Here is the list of the 18 energetic self healing techniques I have offered in this book and suggestions about when is the best time to use each technique.

Mindfulness Meditation Technique

Page 41

This is the basic technique for learning how to work with your attention. The more you practice Mindfulness Meditation the more you will be able to choose where you want to put your attention in the other energetic self healing techniques, and in life in general. This is a good practice to do daily or a few times a week for 5 to 10 minutes.

Connecting to Your Energy Technique

Page 47

This exercise is great for reminding yourself that you have the ability to connect with your energy. Connecting to your energy can be done any time you feel stressed out or too caught up in your thoughts. Use this technique to touch into your energy as a

reminder that there is more to life than what you are worried about in that particular moment.

Raise Your Personal Vibration Technique

Page 56

This is another anywhere and anytime technique - use it whenever you feel you need it. The more you intentionally work with raising your vibration, the more natural it will become to you. If you know you are feeling stuck, depressed, or really just want to make a change, do this technique 2 to 3 times a day for a week or two. You should start to notice a difference.

General All Purpose Energy Clearing Technique

Page 74

This is a very deep and profound healing technique. It is best not to do this technique more than once a day. If you find you are very sensitive to energy clearing, you might even want to limit this

technique to once a week. It is best to give this healing process 20 to 30 minutes of your time and do a thorough energy clearing. If you make this technique part of your weekly self-care routine, you

will find it easier to stay in the flow of life and not become stuck when soul path challenges occur.

Healing Your Column of Light Technique

Page 88

If you know that there has been internal or external emotional abuse in your past, and that your sense of self-love is suffering, this is a very gentle and loving place to heal yourself from. You can spend as little as 5 minutes a day on this technique, or go deeper and make it a 20 minute meditation where you thoroughly clean up your light.

Root Chakra Healing Technique

Page 97

If you know you are struggling with survival issues such as finances, housing, feeling secure in your relationships, then one choice you could make is to focus on healing your Root Chakra. Maybe for one to two weeks focus on doing this meditation daily for around 10 minutes or so. At the end of this time period, you can take a look at your life and evaluate if you see a difference in

your life circumstances. If you feel like more Root Chakra healing is necessary, keep going with this technique. If it feels like a Root Chakra healing has occurred in your life after using this technique, then you can congratulate yourself and move on to another chakra that needs healing.

Sacral Chakra Healing Technique

Page 104

There are many reasons to choose to engage in Sacral Chakra Healing. If you know you want to have more pleasure in your life, you feel your creativity has been blocked, or you want to improve your sex life then you can intentionally choose to work with healing the Sacral Chakra. Choose a 1- or 2-week period to work with this Sacral Chakra Healing Technique for 10 minutes a day. Go gentle with yourself through the process.

Solar Plexus Chakra Healing Technique

Page 108

If you know that you are too hard on yourself and that your own inner self-criticism is hurting you, it is time to focus on the Solar Plexus Chakra. You will need to give yourself around 1 to 3 months to focus on the Solar Plexus if you want to have a real sense that healing has occurred. The Solar Plexus needs a gentle but consistent approach.

Heart Chakra Healing Technique

Page 113

This is a technique to focus on when you know your heart is hurting. When you know you have been hurt by others and by the cruel world in general, and you feel like you have closed up to the world, it is time to focus on the heart. We always want to work slowly, patiently, and compassionately with our heart center. We can't push on the heart. The Heart Chakra Healing Technique could be done for 10 minutes daily, or for a longer period like 30

202

minutes a few times a week. If you find yourself feeling increasingly sensitive when working with the Heart Chakra, that is a sign that healing is occurring.

Throat Chakra Healing Technique

Page 118

This is where you need to focus if you feel like fear and resistance is winning. If you know what you need to do to be happy and be aligned with your purpose but you feel blocked and scared, then it is time to heal past life pain in the Throat Chakra. It might be uncomfortable but if you stick with the changes that start occurring, even if they are confusing, you will get results.

Brow Chakra Healing Technique

Page 122

If you know you are overthinking, worrying, and not listening to your higher self or intuition, it is time to get into the right alignment with your Brow Chakra. This may bring up a lot of

resistance. If you decide to focus on the Brow Chakra Healing Technique, please review Chapter 27 about how the Resistance is Real (page 173).

Crown Chakra Healing Technique

Page 129

Are you ready to surrender your will and your need to micro-manage your life and heal your relationship with Divine guidance? Not everybody is ready to do this. But if you feel like you have not been open to the Divine for a long time, or ever in your life, then this is a daily practice you can do to re-engage with the benevolent forces that are greater than your individual self.

Daily Full Chakra System Healing Technique

Page 136

This is the technique I personally use for my own insomnia. I figure I might as well align my chakras if I am awake! This technique can be done daily as a self-care technique to help keep all our chakras in good form. Or it could be used when you find

yourself feeling stuck, confused, or just feel like you need a general energetic tune-up. Get familiar with the Daily Full Chakra System Healing Technique so you can use it as needed when challenges occur.

Earth Energy Healing Technique

Page 142

This technique can be done as often as you wish. The more we stay open to earth energy the more we stay in the flow of life. Practice this technique until it becomes natural and then do it a few times throughout the day whenever you think of it.

Releasing Stress from the Shoulders Healing Technique

Page 153

This technique can be used whenever you notice you are feeling stressed, specifically in your shoulders. The more you practice this technique the easier it will be to access it when you need it.

205

Pulling in Your Energy Field Healing Technique

Page 161

The best way to work with this technique is to practice it when you are alone and feeling good. Make sure you are somewhere you feel safe, and practice pulling in your energy field a few times in a row. Notice how you feel in your body and mind when the energy field is wide and far from your body, and then in contrast notice how you feel in your body and mind when your energy field is tucked in close to your body. Once you get good at using the Pulling in Your Energy Field Healing Technique you can start using it whenever you are in situations where you are uncomfortable, such as busy places or when you are picking up on someone else's anxious energy.

Letting Go Healing Technique

Page 169

This is another deep healing technique that could trigger emotions, as it can feel very powerful to let go of our past. You can use the

Letting Go Healing Technique as needed, such as when you have a specific issue you want to heal. Ensure you apply compassion and kindness to yourself for the following days after using this technique.

Staying in the Flow Energetic Healing Technique

Page 190

If you feel stagnant in your life or are dealing with chronic depression, this technique can help get your energy flowing again. If your mind is stuck in the past and you find yourself engaged in a lot of blame or resentment, you might need to stick with this meditation 3 or 4 times a week for at least a month to get the energetic flow fully established. If you generally feel you have good flow in your system then use this technique daily or weekly for maintenance.

Appendix Two

Common Issues

This is not a comprehensive list of issues and solutions, but is simply a sample of suggestions I can offer for your use on your healing path.

I encourage you to remember that there are many ways we can heal on our soul path, so please use your common sense when making energetic self healing choices.

Anger Issues

❖ Mindfulness Meditation Technique page 41

❖ Raise Your Personal Vibration Technique page 56

Ankle or Foot Pain

❖ Earth Energy Healing Technique page 142

Apathy

❖ Raise Your Personal Vibration Technique page 56

Broken Heart

Childhood Trauma Healing

Confusion

Depression

Eye Problems

Finding Your Purpose

Hating Your Job

Headaches

Hip Pain

Lack of Self-Love

Life Transitions

Loneliness

Lower Back Pain

Resentment

Sexual Challenges

Stomach Ache

❖ General All Purpose Energy Clearing Technique page 74

❖ Sacral Chakra Healing Technique page 104

Stress

❖ Releasing Stress from the Shoulders Energetic Healing Technique page 153

❖ General All Purpose Energy Clearing Technique Page 74

Let's stay connected!

I have done my best to develop multiple ways we can stay connected so I can continue to provide you with support on your energetic self healing journey.

The information for all of the services I offer can be found listed below and on my website **www.ruthlera.com**

Private Energy Healing Sessions

These sessions are an intimate time for us to work together on your energetic healing by phone or computer video conferencing. In these sessions we work on clearing misinformation in your energy field and chakras. I clear the blockages in the energy field, chakras, vibration, past life soul patterning and any other energy that is ready to be healed. No one can do all of their healing alone. So, please reach out to me or another energy healer for support on your path.

Join the Self Healing Community

This membership program allows you to join in on weekly LIVE calls where we engage in guided energetic self healing techniques together. All members get access to the member-only website

which is packed full of self healing resources such as recorded guided meditations and a dynamic online forum where we support each other on our soul path journeys.

Check Out My YouTube Channel

Many of the meditations I have provided in the book are on my YouTube Channel and I will be continually adding more for your use.

Follow me on Social Media

I am a big user of Facebook and Instagram and an infrequent user of Twitter. I hope we can stay connected through these forums.

Get a Chakra Reading

I love doing chakra readings. When you order a chakra reading I use clairsentience to feel into your chakras and I email you detailed written information about how your chakras are functioning and what changes you need to make for optimum health.

Acknowledgements

I have had so much support in writing this book and it has meant a lot to me.

I've always seen these long lists of acknowledgements in books and have wondered why so many people are being thanked. Now I understand that it truly takes a community to write a book.

Below are just a few of the people whose support has been an essential part of my writing journey, but of course there are so many more people who have encouraged me then I can list here.

I need to thank Vanessa Favero for her enthusiasm and belief in the book, and in me, right from the start of the project. Your assistance in helping me to form my original voice and initial thoughts was a big help.

A huge thank you to Renee Picard for your developmental and copy editing work for the book. Your fresh eye and constant encouragement to be responsive and clear created a more approachable reader experience, which I am very appreciative of.

And thanks to Anna Falcioni for the last minute grammatical editing, and Anne Copland for the proof read.

It is hard to say if this book would even exist if it weren't for Waylon Lewis and his Elephant Journal team. I learned how to share information about meditation and healing effectively through the more than 200 articles they let me submit. Basically, all my business success has come from the connections I have made through the Elephant Journal community, which I am very grateful to be a part of.

Thank you, Adi, for giving me my Kore Story, and for all the studying opportunity you provided for me about what it means to work with a past life story. The vibrational upgrade I received through the receiving of my Kore Story, and the studies that followed, allowed me to come into my power to write this book. You can check out Adi Kanda's work here. http://worldwithoutfear.org/

My original teacher and constant encourager to live beyond the mind is one of my oldest and closest soul friends, Kiran DeJaray. Kiran, you have never stopped explaining to me that I didn't need to listen to my own critical mind, and you never let anyone forget that we are all God. I am continually inspired by the light you shine. You can check out Kiran's teaching and healing work here. http://kirantrace.com/

The thoughts in this book were developed through my friendship with a brilliant, intuitive healer who I've been gifted to have for a soul friend, Kimberlee Fenn. Our long talks while home-schooling

our amazing kids, while simultaneously trying to stay afloat through our busy lives as mothers and wives and aspiring channels for transformation, changed the path of how I know myself to be. I am forever grateful for this time we had together and look forward to more of it in the future.

I also need to thank all of my students and clients. I think some of you have known you have been my guinea pigs for what I've been developing, and you have been so generous with your open-heartedness, allowing me full rein to try out any techniques that inspire me in the name of healing.

You have trusted me and shared honestly with me what has worked for you, and what hasn't, and I really hope you see that your contribution to the development of these energetic self healing techniques has been of benefit to others.

One of my biggest supports has been my land family Colin, Lauren and Teagan, who probably don't even realize how much it means to me that little girls can play any time and any day. It has been a huge source of support to me.

I want to thank my parents, Paula and Alan, for all of their support in helping my family build the beautiful house I get to work in, write in and live in every day.

And of course, the most important people I need to thank are my partner and children. Thank you to my daughter, Anya for always

telling me how cool it is that I am writing a book and cuddling and watching TV with me in the evenings so I can unwind. Thank you to my son, Ensio, for your constant tech support and suggestions, and your kind willingness to always help around the house and yard when I need you.

The biggest thanks of all goes to my life partner, Andy, whose support that I am doing a good job in my work never wavers, and who is left with all the mundane tasks of our life as I hole up in my office for hours, or days at a time, only coming up for air to vent and ask if there is coffee to drink and food to eat, which he swiftly provides. Also, Andy did the formatting and cover for this book- just amazing. I love you so much!

And thank you to all of you for taking the time to read the book. I am sure there have been some parts that resonate with you and maybe others you aren't so sure about. That is perfect with me. Just take what serves you in your healing journey and roll with it. That is all that matters.

About the Author

Ruth Lera is a Mindfulness Meditation teacher, energy healer, natural intuitive, writer, and boreal forest loiterer.

She is also the creator of the Self Healing Community, an online portal for tapping into your innate healing abilities.

Besides being a regular contributor for Elephant Journal, Ruth shares her thoughts on energy healing and the Universe on her blog at **www.ruthlera.com**.

She lives with her partner, two kids, and an assortment of inside and outside animals in Yukon, Canada.

facebook.com/ruthrootawakening/
instagram.com/ruth.lera/
twitter.com/Rlera

Made in the USA
Columbia, SC
23 October 2017